UNDERSTANDING NUMEROLOGY

UNDERSTANDING NUMEROLOGY

The Power to Know Anybody

D. Jason Cooper

The Aquarian Press

An Imprint of HarperCollins*Publishers*

The Aquarian Press
An Imprint of HarperCollins*Publishers*
77–85 Fulham Palace Road,
Hammersmith, London W6 8JB.

First published by The Aquarian Press 1990
First published as *Numerology: The Power to Know Anybody* 1986
3 5 7 9 10 8 6 4 2

D. Jason Cooper asserts the moral right to
be identified as the author of this work

A CIP catalogue record for this book
is available from the British Library

ISBN 1-85538-015-3

Printed in Great Britain by
HarperCollinsManufacturing Glasgow

Dedication

To Sue,
my wife always,
my lover usually,
my proofreader when possible,
my critic when necessary.

CONTENTS

THE PHILOSOPHY OF NUMEROLOGY

Hidden in the forms of our names, in the dates of our birth, in the very words we use, lies a hidden power. To those who know how to tap it, that power reveals us for what we are, and the future for what it shall be.

The study and use of that power is called numerology. It was known to the Babylonians, the Greeks, the Phoenicians, and the Hebrews and can be used by you, today. For though its calculations can be complex enough to need a computer, its basis requires only simple addition. Yet, with the basis alone, you can achieve startling and valuable results in your life.

Numerology

The basis of numerology has been set down by many writers; Greeks such as Pythagoras, Plato, Aristotle, and Xeno; Hebrews like the Sephardic Jews of Spain and Moses, and in modern times, numerology was a part of the teaching of the Hermetic Order of the Golden Dawn, which had among its members such notable figures as Wynn Westcott, S. L. MacGregor-Mathers and W. B. Yeats. Even Nostradamus, in his famous centuries, shows a more than passing knowledge of numerology.

These writers and many others have left us a profound theory of how the universe works. And though the wording may differ from writer to writer or between the Greek and Chaldean (also called Hebrew) schools, and though there may be difference of detail, the mainstream of numerological thought is easily presented and quickly understood.

To numerologists, the universe is based on the *substance behind* what we know as numbers. Now, most writers just say the universe 'is numerical', but in this they forget a numerologist's use of the word is different from the everyday use we've come to accept. You see, to a numerologist, numbers are the expression of the ideas that are the real form of the universe. To them, the universe is made from ideas and ideal forms.

When we see chairs, for example, we are seeing reflections of an eternal, changeless, and ideal chair that exists in the realm of ideas. And the same is true of all other objects: bookcases all reflect an ideal bookcase, televisions an ideal television, and so on.

Even non-physical things are experienced only as a reflection of their ideals. The love we know is only a reflection of eternal love, and so on. All this is consistent with the neoplatonic school of philosophy, but numerologists take the idea and apply it to a practical use.

Numerologists see that each individual number is the representative, the outer form of the primal ideas of existence. So, if we could translate things into their constituent numbers, we could understand their substance and not just their appearance.

In this, the numerologists have moved just one step beyond Plato and his students. Because instead of saying all chairs simply reflect one ideal chair, and all bookcases one ideal bookcase, they have stripped it down even further. They say both are made of the ideals which are seen as numbers, just as computers can build up from a program many different images on a screen.

So, just like a computer's program and its effects, the numerologist knows that nothing in the universe happens by chance. Everything is based on those original ideas. Everything comes from them and goes back to them. Because of this, any one part of the universe can tell us something about every other part.

So let's return to that ideal chair. We can learn about it — or its program if you like — simply by converting the letters of the word 'chair' into numbers, and deriving a single numerical root. Continuing, we could list the various materials a chair can be made of, and examine the numerical equivalents of their names. And we could examine the key elements of certain definitional aspects of a chair, for example, words like sit, object, four-legged, and so on.

We can do the same with your own name, or the names of your friends, or anything else which can be put in terms of music, words, letters, or numbers.

Naturally, some sources we find more useful than others. For example, your house or flat number tells us almost nothing about you, but your name will tell us a great deal. In the course of this book we shall learn exactly how much.

Of Names and Numbers

To a numerologist, each letter has a corresponding number, so that the letters of a word can be converted to numbers and its meaning read. But here the sceptic points to the many alphabets of the world, and the often haphazard way words are developed in a language.

Take differences in language first. In English we use the word 'I' to designate the self, but in German the word is 'ich' and in French it's 'je'. When these are converted by the Pythagorean method into their respective numbers, 'I' becomes 9, 'ich' becomes 2, and 'je' becomes 6.

'There,' says the sceptic, 'the same word in three different languages and it has three different meanings by numerology'.

To which the numerologist can only agree, but then goes on to point out that the difference in numbers simply reflects the different ideals of the self the three different cultures have.

The English-speaking peoples idealize the energetic, optimistic aspect of a person, the doer of the world. They are all cultures that love the person with a broad grasp of things. The German-speaking cultures idealize the collective self. The person who is adaptable and has a modicum of wisdom. It is an essentially feminine aspect which the English-speaking culture often seeks to suppress. The French culture idealizes the self as responsible, as being concerned with the home and family, of operating in cycles (e.g., multiple republics). They see the person as concerned with harmony, balance, and sensuality.

So to the numerologist, the difference between I, ich and je is far more than just what language the word is. Our names at birth, and the entire structure of the language we use is carefully chosen and far from accidental.

The other thing the sceptic can point to is the large number of alphabets in the world, past and present. Apart from the Roman alphabet we use in Western European society, there's the Hebrew, Greek, Cyrillic, Futhark, Chinese, and Japanese alphabets to consider just for a start.

'What', asks the sceptic, 'do you do when you transliterate from one alphabet to another?'

Quite reasonably, the sceptic points to the 'same' letter in different alphabets, and how it is attributed with different numbers. For example, our Roman 'G' is converted to 7 while the Hebrew 'Gimel' and Greek 'Gamma' are both converted to 3.

But, again, a culture carefully, if unconsciously, shapes its letters just as it shapes its words. We should not be surprised that as cultures have developed, so have the alphabets they use and, in tandem with this, the numerological system they use.

It all boils down to seeing if the system that develops is accurate, and this one certainly is.

The Systemata of Numerology

A chart setting out the numerical values of every letter of an alphabet is called a systemata. The systemata used in this book is a modified version of the Pythagorean systemata, shown below.

1	2	3	4	5	6	7	8	9
A	B	C	D	E	F	G	H	I
J	K	L	M	N	O	P	Q	R
S	T	U	V	W	X	Y	Z	

This is the most popular systemata in use today. But though it is very useful, it isn't rich enough to give the full details of a person. For example, note that both I and R are related to 9. In using the Pythagorean systemata, all numbers of a name are reduced to a single digit. For example, Steven is taken as $1 + 2 + 5 + 4 + 5 + 5$ or a sum of 22. $2 + 2$ is 4. Steven is taken as a four. But, if there are Rs or Is in a word, these letters have no effect on the final outcome. That is, row, irowi, rirowir, and wrrirroiiriir all come to exactly two. In short, the systemata reduces two letters to non-existence.

Also, by reducing all values in a word to one digit, it makes no difference, for example, whether a word has an A, S, or J in it. They all mean the same thing.

But, in Hebrew and Greek systemata, these problems were already taken care of. In the Hebrew systemata below, notice how, instead of returning to one, it continues counting by tens and then by hundreds. We'll be seeing later just how important this can be.

English Letter	Hebrew Letter	Name of Letter	Value of Letter
A	א	Aleph	1
B	ב	Beth	2
G	ג	Gimel	3
D	ד	Daleth	4
H	ה	He	5
V	ו	Vau	6
Z	ז	Zayin	7
Ch	ח	Cheth	8
T	ט	Teth	9
I	י	Yod	10
K	כ	Kaph	20
K	ך	Kaph (final)	500
L	ל	Lamed	30
M	מ	Mem	40
M	ם	Mem (final)	600
N	נ	Nun	50
N	ן	Nun (final)	700
S	ס	Samekh	60
O, U	ע	Ayin	70
P	פ	Pe	80
P	ף	Pe (final)	800
Tz	צ	Tzaddi	90
Tz	ץ	Tzaddi (final)	900
Q	ק	Qoph	100
R	ר	Resh	200
S	ש	Shin	300
Th	ת	Tau	400

Of course, the Hebrews gave a different shape and value to five letters when they appeared at the end of a word, and we do not, but the general trend is clear.

In many ways, the Pythagorean systemata was a step backwards for numerologists.

To restore the technology, I began experimentation with what I dubbed the Ulian systemata, and this is given below.

A	B	C	D	E	F	G	H	I
1	2	3	4	5	6	7	8	9
J	K	L	M	N	O	P	Q	R
10	20	30	40	50	60	70	80	90
S	T	U	V	W	X	Y	Z	
100	200	300	400	500	600	700	800	

It took me only a few experiments to realize I had discovered — or rediscovered — something important. And you'll be learning how to make use of that discovery in the rest of this book.

CHAPTER ONE

THE MEANING
OF NUMBERS

The tools of a numerologist are numbers. Without them, everything else is worthless. So, before we go on to anything else, we should first look at the tools of trade.

We'll do this in two steps. First, we'll see the meanings a numerologist attaches to the basic digits, and then we'll use a meditation based on the numbers.

The Numbers

1.

One is the number of the 'universal monad', the number of the beginning of all things. Astrologically, it refers to the Sun and takes on the powers of that planet. Geometrically, it is related to the point.

People with one dominant in their charts take on many of the characteristics attributed to the Sun and the point. They are pioneers, way-showers, people who generate ideas and activity.

These are the people who are self-starters and the self-employed. They tend to be extroverts who like to see others around and tend to enjoy working with the external world rather than concentrating on the introspective aspects of life.

They enjoy building, creating, inventing, and developing. They are people who do well in business, but only in the creative side of things.

Their best areas for careers are advertising, writing, acting, stocks and bonds, real estate development (but not rental); in short, anything where creativity has to be coupled with intuition. For ones, again like the Sun, have a skill with intuition. They seem to just 'smell' the solution to a problem, though they may say — after everything is finished — how they 'worked it out'. For some reason, ones do not like to admit any aspect of intuition aiding their work. This is often heard in the businessman or scientist who claims all their success for 'hard work and thinking things through' or 'careful, scientific study' as if intuition had nothing to do with it. This isn't the case.

Perhaps it derives from the monad or point. The line, plane, and all shapes derive from this. It is the basis for all other elements in geometry. People with one dominant have the same ideal of providing the basis of not only their own work, but the work of others. They want to freely give their ideas to others. Also, they need people around them, to admire them and recognize them as the origin of good things. This is what makes ones prone to self-delusion and Caesarism, for they have a disreputable side. They can become dependent on the opinions of others, and begin to do everything with an eye to 'what others will think'. Worse, they can forget about building, discovering, and creating, and devote themselves to just being flash and flashy. They go to the top spots, the very best restaurants, and the latest shows and always wonder if they'll get 'noticed'.

In love, ones are very generous people. They tend to shower their beloved with as many small presents as they can manage. Rarely big presents, though, just many small ones. Often, the whole life seems to suddenly revolve around the beloved — and he or she is caught in a sudden whirlwind of activity and attention. But just as quickly, the beloved can be dumped. Ones can cool very quickly as a new beloved appears on the horizon. Yet, once they've made a choice, ones settle down rapidly, and turn their attentions to building the family and the home.

About Ones:
Positive Aspects: Energetic, intuitive, enthusiastic, optimistic, creative, generous, gregarious, hard-working.
Negative Aspects: Fickle, egocentric, resentful, prone to self-delusion.
Careers: Business enterprise, writing, advertising, exploring, science, field researcher, salesman, proprietor.

2.

Two is the number of the dyad of Greek geometry, which is the line extending in two directions into infinite space. It is an aspect of 'through any two points there must be one and only one line'. Astrologically, most writers would refer two to the Moon, but this is not correct. Just as the Sun is creativity — the giving of light — that light might be reflected or taken and transmuted.

This latter description is closer to two, and so we refer it to the Earth and the Earth-mother. Remember that when we say the Sun is in Sagittarius, we are also saying that Earth is in Gemini.

In practical terms, this means people with two dominant in their charts are natural born diplomats. They are tactful, adaptable, dependable, patient and understanding. They may not be the self-starters that ones are, but they're steadier.

Twos will finish a project even after their own interest in the matter is at an end. They don't like to leave things unfinished.

Twos aren't very original people, either, but that isn't to say they aren't creative in their own way. Twos hone the ideas that other people create. These are the people who find practical expression of the ideas of others, and who take the various individual ideas of others, hone them like a gem-cutter hones diamonds, puts various ideas together, and comes up with what looks like a whole new idea.

In this, twos are very much like the Earth-mother. She takes the energy of the Sun, the various chemicals in her seas, and creates life. She adds nothing original — she is totally dependent on the Sun for the original power. But what she creates as nature does not look anything like what she received in the first place. This image is very much what twos are about. So it should not be surprising that twos are people who are concerned about the home and children. This is one of the things that keeps twos going — when they've run out of enthusiasm for a project, or a job, they remind themselves about the family or the home, and find they have the strength to keep going for a little while longer at least.

But this principle extends outside just the home. Twos are loyal people, and they are loyal to other people rather than to abstract ideals. They are the sort who support (or vote for) the candidate, not the party.

Their loyalty, their tactfulness, and their forthrightness makes them important to the people they meet. Twos almost always have a wide circle of friends and acquaintances. And often, they are the advisers and confessors for a large number of people. Because as well as being tactful, they tell the truth. Not brutally, 'say and be damned', but with a quiet assurance that often brings people to their side.

This is part of the aspect of the line. The line goes in two directions for an infinite distance. If you could get 'inside' a line, you could then travel to infinity — but only in those two directions.

This is much like the twos. Their options and the options they present others are limited. But they are equally well defined and set. Once two points are set up, the line is fixed.

In the same way, twos know their limits and the limits of others. That is the secret of their wisdom, the wisdom of the Earth-mother.

But twos have their negative side as well. They can become too dependent on others for their ideas, their energy, their leadership. They can become so dependent on a person that they fail to see that the person is going wrong.

Where ones can become gripped by self-delusion, twos are easily gripped by other-delusion. They are the perfect target for the confidence trickster, the salesman, the demagogue.

Twos must take care to be discriminating about what they are being receptive to. If they accept everything wholesale, they will just have a useless and dangerous mish-mash.

Because twos are limited in how much they can accept from others, if they try to take too much, like the Earth accepting too much sunlight, they'll wind up a spiritual desert.

In careers, twos must be aware of both aspects of themselves, and must choose a career that is receptive, which flows in cycles. Things like farming in all its forms, fishing, seasonal work, nursing or medical practice in general. That is where twos do best.

About Twos:
Positive Aspects: Wise, tactful, diplomatic, adaptable, loyal, forthright, patient.
Negative Aspects: Dependent, tends to wishful thinking, can be taken in by others, inactive, blasé.

Careers: Farming, social work, fishing, nursing, medical practice, steward, butler.

3.

Three is the number of the triad, of three points, or the triangle. For any three points there is one plane which will include all of them. But equally, three is taken as the three angles or three sides of the triangle. We will see how this is important in a minute.

Astrologically, three is related to Jupiter, the largest planet in the solar system, and the only planet in the solar system that gives off more energy than it receives from the Sun. Little wonder, with moons that have atmospheres in their own right, that Jupiter is called the sub-solar system.

People with three dominant in their chart have many of the characteristics of Jupiter; good luck, joviality, outgoing attitude, optimism, and a devil-may-care attitude. They even keep Jupiter's fondness for the opposite sex!

Threes are creative, always coming up with ideas, but they're unable to put those ideas into practice by themselves. Threes are, after all, fairly impractical people, and to get the best results, they had best team up with more practical sorts.

Most writers point to threes' creative or artistic nature, but they don't mention that threes are also syncretic. Though they create ideas, they can also add their own ideas to those of others and create a synthesis. This is something threes take great pleasure in.

Because of this, they naturally try to reconcile polarities and to unite opposites. They are people who bridge the new to the old, and make the seam between the two invisible.

One would think this would make them diplomats, and certainly they are full of humanitarian ideals, but like Jupiter, they are full of energy, a star that didn't quite form. They tend, in short, to put foot-in-mouth.

Never mind, they're cheerful and don't take any offence or give any. They're just filled with life.

But, threes don't always alight very well, and rarely build things that last. In this, they are more like the plane-triangle split mentioned earlier.

A plane is getting close to a 'real' object. It exists in two dimensions, and any three points can be contained in a plane. In this, the three is incisive, able to come up with ideas, but not able to put them into action.

Also, three is the triangle, the first regular geometric shape. For the first time, there is a choice of form, and three flits between one and the other.

The ability of three to be creative stems from this choice of method of existence; the boundaries of the possible and the impossible are less well defined than they were for twos. But it is also this that makes them so often unable to put their plans into practice.

In exalting in the changes, threes gain their humanitarian aspects, their love of hospitality. Having freedom themselves, they insist on it for others. And since they have good luck, they see no reason why they can't lend others a hand.

The problems of war and hatred, then, pass threes by. They see no reason why international problems can't be solved like personal problems — by forgiving, forgetting, and having a party.

Their love of everything is infectious, and this gives them a deadly attraction for the opposite sex. The difficulty is, even when threes are serious about the other person (or persons), the partner/s might not realize it. It is common for three's beloved to take things more seriously than threes themselves.

Even when threes are serious, they can't help but do a little flirting, and shall probably have an affair or two, discreetly on the side. Like Montesquieu, if threes aren't with those they love, they love those they are with. And that's just the way they see the world.

About Threes:
Positive Aspects: Enthusiastic, happy, generous, lucky, creative, adaptable.
Negative Aspects: Flighty, chaotic, flirtacious, shallow, unwilling to settle.
Careers: Artist, field officer, business troubleshooter, driver, pilot, professional diver.

4.

Four is the number of the tetrad, which is the cross, the square, or the tetrahedron. So this is the first number with a physical object as one of its symbols, and is therefore the number of the physical self.

Some would say it corresponds to Uranus, but the correct attribution is to Saturn, the father of Jupiter and the symbol of Father Time. This planet had a bad reputation in the Middle Ages as the father of limitations and boundaries, but in fact there's nothing wrong and everything right with having limits, as any four will tell you.

Fours are pragmatic people, very capable of keeping a long-range view in mind — at least during good times. Sometimes, though, they can be plough-ahead sticks-in-the-mud.

Fours are determined people, though, whatever their stage of development. They are people who keep things going and maintain the bureaucratic element in us.

Unlike threes, fours receive no great inspirations. Instead, they apply rigid tests to everything. Every statement, every method of activity must be proved again and again before it can be held to be valid.

These are people who are very much 'on the square'. For just as they require proof from others, they give that proof of themselves. This makes them honest and capable people.

They make excellent lieutenants, but only if they can see themselves as successors when their time comes. In this they differ from twos, who rarely like to be the leader. But more likely, fours will sit, not as king, but as kingmaker. They will sit behind the throne and carefully tend to the daily business of getting the taxes in and keeping expenditure down to a reasonable level. In this, fours are aided by a careful attention to detail. Part of their need to get positive proof is the denial of the use of big assumptions. Everything must be as closely argued as possible.

Fours also like order, and this often means no more than a simple dislike of change, which can lead to the leaden and sedentary aspects of some fours.

These are people who don't like change just because it is change, and they don't care if it is change for the better. They can be not just conservative, but traditionalist in the extreme. They can also become the sort of people who just love to do factory work. The idea of operating in machine-like capacity, repeating tasks endlessly, can appeal to some fours.

Most, however, prefer a bit more variety than that. They would be happier in a guild or tradesman capacity, where some form of creativity can come to the fore. Fours may not be original, but they like to make things and they like to show their skill in doing so.

The astrological association to Saturn provides some further clues about this number. Saturn was the outermost planet known in ancient times, and represented the outer bounds of human abilities. In the same way, fours deal with those aspects of life that can't be avoided. The problems of overseeing, of control, of meting out demands that are greater than the capacity to supply.

Like Saturn, four does not create so much as it reallocates in a careful way. It is a measuring rod that keeps all things in balance.

Geometrically, the same message comes through in other ways. Four is represented as the cross, the square, and the tetrahedron. As the cross, it is the symbol of the world, and so the symbol of natural order and natural processes.

The square has much the same meaning, but is taken more generally as the physical world. Most importantly, it is the aspect of our physical selves, our bodies, our methods of doing things.

Interestingly, the tetrahedron is a three-dimensional figure, being four triangles joined at their sides. It is this, connected to one of the symbols of three, that puts it in a higher order, just as Saturn was Jupiter's father. It therefore represents the realm of physical space that we occupy, and returns four again to representing the world.

It should not be surprising then, to find that fours are very good at making money, whether in business, by marriage, or by inheritance. Money is something they can make in prodigious quantities. They are also people who enjoy physical comfort. They keep their luxuries around them, and find a few necessary to keep life bearable.

About Fours:
Positive Aspects: Hard working, industrious, agile, keeps the long-run in mind, logical.
Negative Aspects: Stick-in-the-mud, repetitious, dull, unimaginative.
Careers: Financial investor, financial adviser, executive, craftsman, factory worker.

5.

Five is the number of people, as individuals or as a species. It is astrologically associated with Mercury, the messenger of the Greek gods. Geometrically, it is related to the five-pointed star, the pentagram, and with the pentagon.

The things that distinguish fives are that they are great travellers and great tricksters. But as travellers, fives are people who are tourists rather than emigrés. They travel to a place for a while, and then return home. They are the short-range travellers of numbers.

As tricksters they are not just practical jokers, but people who skip and hop from one idea to another, one loyalty to another.

Five is an enthusiastic number. They will give anything new a chance, they will try anything untried. And just like twos who accept any influence, fives can try anything new without thinking about it. And that, unfortunately, can be drugs or crime as quickly as new theories of physics.

Fives can be in danger of being a jack-of-all-trades, master at none. But for all that, they escape being shallow because they link up the various things they study.

Fives will take many small ideas from a large range of other people, put them together, and then put them forward in an eclectic whole. Often, the whole is put together like a jigsaw puzzle, but the individual pieces are still all recognizable. Unlike twos, fives do not hone the ideas they get from others. Unlike ones and threes, they aren't creative or original.

But the talents fives have of observation and synthesizing the ideas of others can be very valuable. As leaders they don't ram their ideas down the throats of others, but accept the ideas of others. At the end, even the lowest in the hierarchy can feel they have made some contribution to the whole effort.

This makes fives good magazine editors, research assistants, academics, salesmen — especially travelling salesmen, roadies, actors, and entrepreneurs. In fact, anything where the five can constantly vary the method of attack, keep doing something new, while aiming at one goal. This is where fives will do well.

As I said before, fives are observers. They look the world over, and that has a lot to do with their desire to travel. But it also gives them a gift of the gab. They like to talk and are good listeners as well. They are great conversationalists.

In this they are very like Mercury. He was a traveller, a story-teller, the inventer of the lyre. In the same way, fives today do much the same things. They enjoy music, change, and activity.

Mercury is also the planet of adolescence, the time when people are most receptive to change and most able to live with changes made. Fives keep that spirit long after adolescence has left them.

But it also makes fives unfixed. They have little tradition to fall back on. They always have to ad lib what they are doing, even if a perfectly good way of doing things is at hand. This makes them use up a lot of energy they need not otherwise use. More, it can make them flighty, fidgety. They can become hyperactive and garrulous. This is the great danger for fives; they need to be anchored down.

Fives themselves take on a protective colouring in the company of others, just as Mercury is the master of disguise. This makes them bad advisers, because they will always feed back to a person what they think that person wants to hear. It also makes it hard for them to ask advice, since they will also ask what they think a person wants to be asked. This isn't lying — though many fives are capable of that. It's just a natural part of the camouflage that fives find vital to their sense of self.

Geometrically, this is the number of the pentagon and the pentagram. Notice how, after four, the number of choices is restricted again, and that here there is no three-dimensional form.

Five is the number of Man, and the number of passing time. It is the number which, with four's three-dimensional space, creates the matrix of our universe. Hence the pentagram, which looks like a person with legs spread, arms outwards, and head in the topmost point.

But pentagrams can also be inverted, with one point downwards. This is a symbol of evil, and it is in time, where change is first possible, that free will and choice are made. Only in time can things be changed for the better or the worse. This is something that underlies the observation of fives, and their camouflage.

About Fives:
Positive Aspects: Quick witted, friendly, adventurous, exploratory, intelligent.
Negative Aspects: Deceitful, garrulous, hyperactive, hypocritical, unable to participate, indecisive.
Careers: Musician, magazine or newspaper editor, librarian, researcher, academic, salesman.

6.

Six is the number of harmony, the number of the cube, the hexagon, and the six-pointed stars — the two forms of the hexagram. Astrologically, it is referred to the Moon, or Luna, the planet of equilibrium between light and dark, of all things having their place in the cycle of events.

Here, again, the geometry is diversifying, and again, we have a three-dimensional form. But, this is connected to four, not five. This leaves five somewhat alone, and links four and six. So, like four, six is a steady influence on people. People with six dominant in their charts are patient, steady, and capable. In this, they are like fours, but for sixes, everything revolves around the home. This is not just the home in the narrow sense, but in the sense of the home, family, dynasty, and life-style. All fit together for sixes into a single concept.

Sixes are concerned with people, and loyal to people whereas fours are a bit more loyal to processes. This makes sixes good people to have around wherever the growth of people is important. That includes areas such as teaching, social work, politics, child-minding, medicine, being parents, and so on.

However, sixes in groups often get stuck with being the workhorses. They are sometimes too willing to do things or give things up for other people. Sixes have too much of a tendency to forget about themselves. When they finally do remember, it's too late. Then they can be resentful and destructive. For just as sixes do not forget favours, they don't forget slights, either, and they can be revengeful.

Sixes can also become pernickety. They are people who pay attention to detail, and they can demand this in others when it really isn't necessary or desirable. They can, in fact, tend to retreat from others in the guise of teaching. This sort of six is the compulsive cleaner or the persistent nagger. The people who lose the big picture in a welter of detail.

But at their best, sixes are charming hosts. Their homes and activities always seem to be well ordered. They move with grace and style, and always have an eye on the latest fashions and trends. They are well organized, and make excellent team leaders in any situation.

Astrologically, the planet of sixes is the Moon, the planet of the triple goddess. As Diana, she is the chaste virgin huntress. As Ceres or Selene she is the fertile harvest mother. As Hecate she is the dark temptress and ravager of lonely travellers. She can place any one of her faces towards others, and this lends a certain mystery to her. Many people may meet sixes, but very few see all their sides. Sixes are often aware of this, but rarely use it in the way a one or five might use it.

Sixes attract others by always having that bit extra that is to be discovered. But sixes are not flirts — like threes. Their plans, right from the beginning, tend to centre around finding somebody suitable and settling down with them. The sixes of the world are faithful and tend to keep things in a marriage alive by always having something apparently new to offer. I say apparently because sixes are creative, but tend to keep ideas stocked up. They don't let them all out at once or as soon as they come into six's head (rather like Diana, who kept a quiver full of arrows).

This same sort of association occurs with the geometrical aspects of the number. Six is harmony, just as the six-pointed star can also be two triangles perfectly balanced. But six has other manifestations, too. It is also the cube, a six-sided figure made of squares. Remember that the square was a symbol for four, but that the three-dimensional symbol was the four-sided tetrahedron. We therefore have a double link between the two numbers that excludes five. In this, six is like Hecate, who was goddess of the crossroads. It was Hecate who isolated travellers at night, trapped them, and slew them. Like sixes today, Hecate never forgave a slight. She was a goddess of vengeance, but a goddess of justice as well. She was never petty, but simply saw to it that things were kept to rights.

The six is also related to the hexagon, which is the shape of the cells of honeycombs. This is related to the fertility aspect of the number, to Ceres and Selene. Again, in association with bees, sixes are concerned with order and progeny.

The uniscursial hexagram is a six-pointed star which can be drawn without lifting the pen from paper or re-tracing any lines. I've drawn one below.

This is a symbol for six that has emerged only this century. Its full purpose is not yet known, but it relates to the system of cycles itself. The seasons, the cycles of life from birth to death, reincarnation, and so on.

About Sixes:
Positive Aspects: Industrious, strong willed, concerned about others, harmonious, graceful.
Negative Aspects: Vengeful, too self-sacrificing, pernickety, nagging.
Careers: Teacher, lawyer, social worker, child-minder, doctor, nurse, farmer.

7.

This is the number of mysticism and, again, a change in symbols. It is the number of two seven-pointed stars, or heptagrams, the heptagon, and of the triangle within a square.

Astrologically, it is the number of Venus, the goddess of mysteries, and the planet shrouded in cloud.

Where sixes are people who are involved with others, sevens are people one step removed from the world. They are not only natural philosophers, but mystics and poets as well.

They are, like fives, people who observe the world. But unlike fives, they don't don camouflage or disguise and get involved in the world at the same time. Instead, they remain apart. They are not people who tell others what they have seen. Mind you, they do keep their confidences, and are people who keep their promises. But what they observe or are told, they keep as a store of wisdom.

Sevens are thinkers, and being one step removed from the hustle and bustle, they can take on an air of unworldliness. Sometimes this comes to no more than an absent-mindedness, at other times a real and obvious ability to perceive beyond the obvious.

Nor do they become involved in the rounds of parties, discos, and trend setting. If they let their hair down, it is as an exemplary artist; a musician, a composer, painter, sculptor, or writer.

But sevens don't create ideas as much as they gather ideas from some universal pool. They have access to the storehouse of ideas from which all ideas have to come originally. You see, sevens are introspective as well as intuitive. A one never knows where the ideas he or she gets comes from. A seven knows. Sevens continue to explore themselves and their internal worlds. Sevens tend to believe that by looking within themselves they can derive the fundamental description of the universe they seek.

But sevens can also fail to understand the world. And rather than just be distant from it, they can hide from it. In this, sevens can turn inward to such an extent they never come to apply what they perceive, or apply it in a very lop-sided fashion. They can put on rose-coloured spectacles which they would never take off again. They may be wise in most ways, but they can fall for the idea that, 'if ignorance is bliss, then 'tis folly to be wise'.

Sevens are sometimes lonely people, unable to understand how to use the time they need alone. Instead they come to think there is something 'wrong' with them and they should be more outgoing. Or they begin to think they don't need people at all, and become recluses.

Neither is good for the sevens of the world.

Astrologically, the planet of seven is Venus, the goddess of Mysteries. In ancient Greece and Rome, there was an understanding that not all knowledge was intellectual in nature. Some was knowledge it took a special knack or talent to have. This was called gnosis. Sevens are people who understand the importance of gnosis. Even when they don't possess it, they do understand its importance.

Geometrically, we are entering an area where the symbolism is becoming more and more complex. Suffice to start with the symbol for seven as a triangle in a square. The triangle represents spirit, the square the physical body. As a whole it is the living body, a body infused with spirit. It is also, by the way, the symbol of the Tarot cards.

Whenever drawn, the triangle is not allowed to touch the square at any point. This is to signify that soul or consciousness is independent of the physical body. It just inhabits the body. The method of this inhabitation, however, is symbolized by another seven-sided figure — the heptagram.

The seven-pointed star provides the symbol of the seven days of the week. The seven planets of antiquity; the seven metals; the seven ages of creation, and so on. It was a symbol of the Mysteries, the secret knowledge that would allow someone to know the important elements of the universe. This, in essence, is the message of the number seven, and what its messengers bring to us.

About Sevens:
Positive Aspects: Perceptive, truthful, keeps confidences, wise, observant.
Negative Aspects: Absent-minded, shy, sluggish, unable to cope with the world, secretive, foolish.
Careers: Artist, dancer, commentator, clerk, academic, scientist, tarot reader and diviner.

8.

Eight is a very powerful number. Geometrically it is two interlaced squares or the eight-pointed cross, the octagon and the octagram. Astrologically, it is related to Pluto, the last-discovered planet, and the planet of sex, death, and regeneration.

Eights are born organizers and born leaders. Most are able not only to set goals for people, but to keep the group together long enough for it to do what the eight wants it to do. For, sad to say, they are not only good organizers, they can be quite manipulative. Machiavelli had nothing on them.

This isn't to say eights are egotistical — like some ones. Quite the opposite, eights can work happily in the lower echelons of an organization, but they must have two prerequisites. First, they must see themselves as being able to rise in the organization on merit. Second, they must agree with the goals set by the organization or have such respect for superiors that eight goes along happily.

Then eights show how very hard and ably they can work. And, strange to tell, it often doesn't seem to matter to an eight what the organization is for. It can be a business, a charity, a sports club, an association, a union, or a political party; quite often just making the organization grow and succeed is enough.

But with this organizational ability is a strong sense of justice and a thorough knowledge of self. Eights do not act blindly, they know what they are doing. They don't push themselves or those around them too hard if they can help it. And, with a sense of justice, they make certain everyone carries their load without shirking. And double the order for the eights involved. The problem is, sometimes they set such a cracking pace, they don't always notice when others are starting to fall behind.

Also on the bad side, eights can be single-minded. They can bet so often on themselves that they burn their ships too often. They can then bet everything on themselves and lose. Even worse, they can blame others for not putting enough of an effort in. They just forget that what they were asking for not everyone can provide. Fortunately, this isn't done often. Many eights are successful in what they do.

Astrologically, eights are referred to the planet Pluto. This planet is the planet of sex and death, and the regeneration (or reincarnation) that reconciles them. So eights are able to look at things and, like threes, cut to the heart of the matter. But where threes are inspired, eights can see the pattern. They know how they got to the heart.

They also have a certain compulsive ability to attract the other gender. They know it, and sometimes they use it. Yet, not often. They take their love very seriously, and don't give it readily. So there is little to fear from them — they will seek a definition of the relationship before it starts.

Eights can see into the universe. Unlike sevens, though, eights have a slightly more magical than mystical view of things. They see the universe as a living thing of itself rather than a body that spirit infuses. They respect that living thing, and they learn its laws. By doing so, eights can be psychic, and they use their hunches and perceptions to great effect.

Geometrically, eight has a number of symbols, but all refer back to the same basic meaning; self. The octagon, for example, is recognized by Jungian psychologists as a symbol of the self.

The eight-pointed star is also a symbol of self. But, as two equal-armed crosses set with a common centre at 45° from each other (+ and ×) it is a symbol of the self in balance. It is a symbol of being able to reach all the primal parts of one's 'self', and to be able to use them.

The octagram, an eight-pointed star made from one continuous line, repeats the message, but is a symbol of the dynamic self; the self growing and acting upon the world. This is eight, very much, acting upon the world and learning from that.

About Eights:
Positive Aspects: Determined, leadership abilities, intelligent, foresighted, organizing, just, industrious.
Negative Aspects: Unforgiving, calculating, does not take the weakness of others into consideration, not spontaneous.
Careers: Business investor, proprietor, politician, general, soldier, adviser.

9.

This is the last of the primary numbers, and the greatest visionary among them. Its geometric symbols are the enneagram and enneagon and three interlaced triangles. The interlaced triangles, by the way, are the symbol of numerology.

Astrologically, it refers to both Mars and Neptune. These are the astrological planets of curiosity and understanding, and the magical view of the world.

As I said, nines are visionaries. They understand that the universe operates in cycles, and that by using those cycles they can achieve what they want. But nines temper what they want by estimating what they can have without disturbing the balance of the universe. Balance is a concept very important to them.

Nines are intuitive, and often their visions of the future are incredibly accurate. However, their visionary element also makes them want to improve things. They sincerely want to better the lot of their fellows. But, this improvement doesn't just mean giving someone a meal, or money, or the means of obtaining meals. Nines are aware of the substance that lies behind the universe, and realize that what we receive in life is essentially what we deserve to receive. So, nines seek to discover what the substance is when it is not being universal but personal. That is what I mean when I say nines have a magical view of the world.

Like many visionaries through the ages, nines often travel. In this they are like fives. But where fives travel short distances, nines are the great emigrées of the world. When they travel, they spend months meeting the local people, learning about their ideas and ways of life, and from observing this, learning about life.

Like threes, nines are happy-go-lucky. But like sevens, nines have an element of reserve, some part of themselves they don't readily give to others. None-the-less, nines are also prone to fail to see that others may not hold their views. There's an evangelical streak to nines that makes them believe whatever they believe at any one time is what everyone should believe. Worse, they can't understand why other people can't understand the true nature of things. They therefore have great trouble understanding the motivations of other people. Also, knowing the final outcome of things, nines sometimes act as if it has happened. That is, they push things along too quickly and suffer the backlash that is the inevitable result.

There is also a self-destructive element in nines. In learning about themselves, they begin to test themselves. This they often do to destruction. They also test things around them too much; relationships, ideas, lovers, everything. But nines are people who live by oaths, so at least their word can be trusted.

They are gregarious people, within their limits. They enjoy a good party, and are sometimes over-fond of drink especially. They can also tend to get fat in their middle age, because they enjoy sweets.

As to their relationships, they see these not so much as one-to-one but rather as a group. So it's not 'me and the spouse and the children', it's 'we the family'. Nines are experimental lovers, too. Part of the testing and their desire to know everything there is to know about the beloved.

Astrologically, nine is related to two planets, and is the only digit to be so honoured. The first planet is Mars, which most people know as the planet of war. Yet Mars deals with a wide variety of events; agriculture, the state of *civitas*, the law, curiosity, masculinity. But, it is curiosity, the desire to know, which is most easily recognized as a trait of nine.

The other planet is Neptune, the planet named after the god of the seas. The associations of undercurrents, secrets, and hidden powers relates very well to nines. Most of them have secrets they keep even from those closest to them, and all nines enjoy a bit of cloak-and-dagger in their lives.

Nines also have a certain reserve power they can draw on if they have to. This, again, is as much a part of their Martian character as their Neptunian one. Just like a seed forming on a mature plant, so nines develop themselves in ways we don't really understand.

Geometrically, three interlaced triangles are nines' most important symbol. These symbolize the balancing and equalizing of various forces. This is important to nines, because sometimes they seek to grasp so much they can easily dissipate themselves. Nines can wind up trying to travel in all directions at once.

The balancing of forces is important as a way of setting the world to rights. To them, all evil stems from imbalance, and just to fight evil is to take everything one stage too late.

About Nines:
Positive Aspects: Humanitarian, broad-minded, just, spiritually minded, artistic.
Negative Aspects: Conceited, sly, devious, power-hungry, hasty, gluttonous.
Careers: Writer, business executive, small shop owner, cleric, magical order adept, gardener.

Such are the primary numbers as used by numerologists. In addition, most modern numerologists use 11 and 22 as if they were single-digit numbers. For those who wish to do likewise, I include the following descriptions.

11.

Symbolized by the eleven-pointed star, eleven is generally associated with Uranus. Its prominence in a person's chart provides them with skills in the psychic and the occult, and a pronounced inclination to the secret. This is a number of spiritual insights.

Idealistic and visionary, there is in elevens a strong streak of the sceptic. Material proof demands intuitional agreement. Inspiration demands material proof. This is a hard creed to live by, but it is the ideal elevens stand for.

But this and a desire to seek out their own way often makes elevens into the eccentrics of the world. Some see the flouting of conventions as a way of seeking truth, but others see it simply as a way to get others excited. These people fall for every new fad, creed, cult, or trend. They just throw themselves into first one thing and then another. Often, in older age, this can lead to elevens being dejected. Everything is a banal hollow existence. The sorrow Buddha spoke of, but not the joy he taught the sorrow would give way to.

Nevertheless, elevens are always ready to share their thoughts with others. When they speak, they do so from the heart with a leavening of inspiration. In ancient times they would have been natural prophets, augurers, or priests. Today clerics, councillors, and willing friends are their allotted roles.

However, elevens aren't a soft touch to anybody. When faced with the troubled, elevens could just as easily offer help in return for improvement. Elevens, it must be remembered, often have great power over others. To have this power, they have to explore themselves. This is what successful elevens do — meticulously, like a bird preening feathers. They are the people who have their horoscopes done, learn to do their numeroscopes, and so on. They always test themselves, find their weaknesses, and work on them. If they fail to do this, they may only half-perceive their faults. Usually they project their own failings onto the rest of the world. That's when elevens can become very dangerous. They seek to impose their own sick wills on the rest of the world. It's like a person discovering they have a sweet tooth and barring any sweets from their house. It would be better to overcome the sweet tooth.

Elevens can be very charming people. They make others feel important. Though they're magnetic, they remain very loyal to those close to them.

Uranus makes elevens mystics and subject to strange visions. Elevens often perceive what others can't and so become creative in a way twos are not. They don't create ideas, but hone those they take from the natural store of the universe.

In this store they have unlimited credit. This makes them good artists of any sort, doctors, scientists (scientists do best when they work with inspiration), and teachers of new ways.

Where elevens fail most often is to keep up their efforts when victory or the goal is in sight. They don't follow through often enough, and this often leads to frustration, embarrassment, and worse.

Elevens should heed their own advice more often, and see that everyone in the world receives exactly what they deserve to receive.

About Elevens:
Positive Aspects: Inspirational, humanitarian, charming, mystic, patient, listens to others.
Negative Aspects: Projects own faults on others, can't take criticism, lazy.
Careers: Cleric, councillor, artist, diplomat, politician, teacher of the new age.

22.

This is the number most writers would attribute to the planet Neptune. Geometrically, it has never been linked with any symbol. No doubt, however, two eleven-pointed stars interlaced could be used.

Twenty-twos are people who are masters of their own environments. Their homes are, as much as possible, carefully constructed to match their personalities.

They are imaginative and secretive, but less intuitive than most people (themselves included) would believe. Instead, their subconscious and conscious minds combine to use a tightly controlled logic.

These are people who are attuned to their subconscious needs and impulses and are able to accept them. Because of this, they understand the storms and currents that can arise from its depths. This self-knowledge allows them to understand the unstated needs, drives, and ambitions of others.

In some, this creates a heavy-handed cynicism. They always see the 'ulterior motive' for their own and others' actions. What they forget is that everybody has multiple motives for doing anything, and that nobody is so simple that an unstated motive cannot be found for anything we do. Cultural convention, it must be remembered, makes us pick one of our motives as 'the' motive. And if the cynical twenty-twos of the world can realize this they quickly become much happier.

The optimists of the twenty-twos are builders and givers on a grand scale. We should remember that Neptune was not only the god of the stormy deep, but of life-giving water. The Greeks accredited him with giving humanity the horse, one of the most valuable things in Greek civilization. Thus, many twenty-twos concentrate on selflessness, joy, and the creativity inherent in human beings.

The cynical twenty-twos, if the truth be told, build things halfway and then tear them down again. They are afraid of being found out as less than perfect. It is a false fear, but one that overtakes the cynics.

The optimists, on the other hand, build constantly. They fortify themselves with reason, by building a logical worldview. They establish strong and lasting relationships, especially within the family, and they build themselves a career.

They become architects, builders, designers, engineers, but also, builders in a less concrete way, they are teachers, camp councillors, clerics, writers, and are found in any field where building is important.

The essential character of twenty-twos is the wish to leave behind a world just slightly better for their having been here. Luckily for us many of them succeed.

About Twenty-Twos:
Positive Aspects: Industrious, creative, builder, loyal, logical, supportive, insightful, optimistic, generous.

Negative Aspects: Cynical, pessimistic, manipulative, does not complete tasks.

Careers: Engineer, architect, factory worker, organizer, developer, landscaper, designer, clerk, secretary.

Such are the basic numbers as used by most modern numerologists. It is best that you learn these meanings, but not be slavishly tied to them. Numbers are living things, and it is best if you treat them that way and let your understanding of them grow over time.

This will make it much easier when you have to do a numeroscope and have to analyse complex numbers like 1241, which has as specific a meaning as the double-digit numbers eleven and twenty-two. To aid this understanding, I provide below a meditation on the primary numbers.

The Meditation

If you are not certain what I mean by meditation, don't worry. I'm referring to no more than organizing a train of thoughts so they all centre on a common theme. There are other forms of meditation, of course, but we needn't go into them here. For now, you should understand this is not going to be much different from getting deeply involved in a book you are reading.

To begin, you should find a comfortable place where you can sit or lie down without being disturbed. Any tight, restricting clothes you have, such as belts or shoes, should be removed.

Once you are comfortable, begin to relax your muscles. Just say to yourself that you will relax. Begin with, 'I will now relax the muscles in my left leg. My muscles are beginning to relax. The tension is now magically flowing out of them. The muscles in my left leg are now relaxed.' Then do the right leg, the left arm, and so on.

It doesn't matter if your muscles don't completely relax to begin with. In time they will relax in an instant just by saying to yourself, 'Time to relax'.

Once that's done, close your eyes and imagine a point.

Now, this point has no mass, weight, height, width, or depth. It's merely a position in space. It's just a concept that doesn't exist in the real world.

You can't even think of it as a dot. It is just represented by a dot. It is a nothing that exists.

And yet, you should begin to feel it exuding power. This, after all, is the primary element of geometry. From this comes all else. This is the origin of things.

Feel the energy it gives off, and let it pour that energy through you. Imagine your whole body glowing a golden warm.

This is the concept of one. It exists by itself, and so doesn't interact with others. It has power and creativity.

Just keep the image and play with the concepts of the number one as you know them, but link each concept with this image.

When you've done that, shift the position of your mind's eye. Imagine yourself moving around ninety degrees, and discovering you weren't looking at a point at all. It was in fact a line — a line that went straight through you.

This is a different matter, now. Though a line has no weight or mass, it does have one dimension. Depending on the direction the line is drawn (or your point of view), this can be height, width, or depth.

Think of that for a while. Shift the line in your imagination. Let it be all three dimensions one at a time.

See the power you felt before as a series of pulses along the run of the line. This is the number two. The power is received, and like twos, the line is dependent. Yet it is a figure that reaches into infinite space.

If you were inside the line, trapped tightly and able to move only along the line, would you say you had infinite freedom? Think about it. For isn't this the acceptance of limitations that twos are noted for?

Think about the various elements of two, and relate each of them back to this original vision.

Now, shift your viewpoint again. Move upwards and see that it was not a line, but a plane that kept in scheme with you.

It's the second time you were fooled. It should make you wonder what, on this trip, you can be certain of. What geometrical concepts can you hold to?

This is a plane. It goes in two dimensions out to infinite distance. Utterly flat and without variation.

Imagine yourself standing on it. It is a plane that bisects the little universe we've been exploring. You on one side, everything else on the other.

But if you could ride the plane, how much more freedom you would have than you have in the line. Indeed, more freedom than in your daily life.

But you could not reach even a speck beyond the other side of the plane. Everything would be seen, and nothing would be obtainable.

But you could always think about it, and be creative in ideas. So a three is creative, but unable to put most plans and ideas into practice.

Though you have developed great freedom in your mental images, you are still restricted. You can build very little. Again, like a three.

Complete those concepts. Draw each of them to the image of you standing on the plane which divides infinity into two.

Notice how the three points on the plane can be seen as glowing with the same power that the original point had. Notice how the power isn't diminished for the tripling of numbers.

Watch as the golden glow stretches to form a triangle from the three points. This is the other symbol for three.

Watch as the triangle fills in, until it is all glowing golden. Now, flow through it. Let yourself gently fall into the other side of the plane.

See that you've fallen into a tetrahedron. A set of four triangles sealed at the edges. Feel its walls, how they feel warm. This is a symbol of four. It is three-dimensional space. It is structure and order. It is the number four.

Let the four triangles of the tetrahedron move away from you, expanding forever until they cease to exist.

Exist, alone, in the universe. No stars, no worlds, not even time, just empty space.

This is what four fears — and fear is something you should realize is created by choice. Fours have reached the 'other side' of the plane and they now have to order the things they have found.

But there is nothing on the other side. The plane was just a mirror.

Imagine a square forming in front of you. This is four as matter. Existence. This is the world, for we have ordered chaos, and in so doing banished all else.

Now, we are almost at reality as we know it.

Think about this. The well-spring of ideas has been used up. Now there is only using what was thought to be there. This is four as we know it.

Relate each idea you have about four to this concept, this image of the retreating tetrahedron and the square.

Now, see in the square the stars and galaxies and planets. See it in all detail. Focus in on our galaxy, our solar system, our world, and yourself doing this exercise.

In your mind's eye, but physically if you wish, spread your arms out sideways, so that they reach out straight. Spread your legs. This should make you look a little like a five-pointed star, a pentagram.

Imagine a pentagram formed around you, and a line drawn from point to point, making a pentagram within a pentagon. This is you as a human being within the symbol of humanity.

Now, riding on the pentagram/pentagon, fall through the square and enter the universe. See how the various stars grow and die, how they finish as novae. See the planets swarm about the stars. See, in short, the development of time.

This is our universe in time. This is the highest order of infinity we can know. And it has taken us halfway through the primary numbers before we reached our universe. Everything else had an element of abstraction to it.

Is it any wonder, then, that fives have to see everything, and often have to try things out?

And, think about fives as people who wear masks. Little wonder when we stop to think of it. They have to see everything from every point of view.

Examine each of the concepts you have about five, but in the light of the universe as a whole, as something that is within you as much as you are within it.

Let the pentagram and the pentagon vanish. Let yourself in your mind's eye and, if necessary, physically, drop your arms and bring your legs together. Stand before the universe.

Notice how six stars glow much brighter than the others. Notice how lines form between certain of the stars until two interlaced triangles are formed. This is the six-pointed star — two interlaced triangles of equal force balanced one against the other.

In Medieval symbolism, one triangle stood for darkness, the other for light. Others have written that one stands for fire, the other for water. Whatever, the two triangles represent two separate and opposing forces of equal strength, each contending against the other in a dialectic.

This would imply that the goal of things is not victory of one side over the other, but the contest itself. Reflect on this in its various forms.

Notice that the Moon waxes exactly as much as it wanes. Think about sports teams you support: do you want them never to be in danger of losing? Does it not imply the acceptance of the 'other side' in things? Seeing what the other side sees?

Is this not very much what six is about, as a number?

Notice also that the first five numbers were basically about developing structure. These higher numbers are very much numbers about morality and life lessons.

Contemplate the various things you know about six, and lead them all back to the concept of two finely balanced forces. Two seemingly antagonistic forces that in reality need each other to survive.

Let the downwards-pointing triangle fade, and a square form again, just like the one through which you first saw the universe. Don't let the triangle touch the square at any point.

This is the symbol of seven. This is spirit within matter. It is having entered through the plane and found the source of ideas in the self.

Contemplate this in the light of the various attributes of the number seven. The mysticism, the reserve from others. Let each idea be connected to that symbol.

But also, contemplate it within yourself. See how you are spirit within matter. A consciousness within a body.

There is a universe within you, and one without you. This is the source of your ability to understand things. If there is not an element of it within you, you will never contemplate or know the thing itself.

For instance, you know the opposite sex only through your animus or your anima. The animus is the little male inside all females, and the anima is the little female inside all males.

At this stage of your meditation, you can call on your counterpart for understanding, wisdom, and advice.

Contemplate on each of the elements of the meaning of seven, and relate them to this one image of a person asking advice and help from their counterpart.

Now examine the triangle within the square again, and watch as the triangle changes and forms itself into a square, such that the two squares interlace.

This is the nature of eight as we most often know it. Two forces, one operating on the other. In this it is like the two triangles, but without the direction the triangles imply.

One force succeeds over the other. Absolute failure or absolute success. This is a description of the polarity of opposites, where six was the polarity of complements.

Only one person can own a certain piece of land. Only one person's view prevails.

Yet, watch as energy draws lines from point to point on the squares. Watch as the squares vanish, leaving an octagon. This is a universally-recognized symbol of self. There is not the struggle of the two triangles. Instead we have a symbol of self in contemplation.

A very different thing than before.

Again, watch as an eight-pointed star forms within the octagon. And again as lines form to directly link every third point. This forms an octagram or eight-pointed star as the original star, the double cross, vanishes.

The whole describes eight as various elements of self trying to come to the fore. The winning element must show itself stronger and more useful than the others.

This is the force of evolution, of learning.

Examine your knowledge of eight in this light. See how the struggle teaches what works and what does not. Link each aspect of your knowledge of eight to the system of succeeding symbols.

Note that in this case and this case only, it is not the symbol or the symbols themselves you are linking your knowledge to. It is the fact of succession itself.

Let the panoply stop, and view three interlaced triangles in perfect balance.

This is nine, the overcoming of the struggle itself by knowing the meaning of the struggle. The three triangles represent the balance of forces, but not forces that struggle to neutrality.

Instead, they are forces that operate in cycles. It is the Moon being full in its time, or of every person having their day. Everything must come in its own time and in its own way, and this is very much the message of nine.

Consider your knowledge of the number, every fact and concept, in the light of the image of the three triangles. Link each individual fact to the idea of three forces equalling each other and so succeeding each other over time.

You will now be ready to come out of your meditation. To do so, say to yourself, 'My meditation is completed. I will open my eyes and go forth healthier, happier, and wiser than I was before.' Then open your eyes and flex your muscles.

Keep a record of your thoughts and impressions during this meditation. You will be surprised how much it can help your knowledge of numerology.

CHAPTER TWO

THE NUMEROSCOPE

A horoscope is a map of the zodiac as seen from any one part of the earth at any one time. So, from a birthdate, an astrologer learns about a person from that map. Numeroscopes do the same thing for the numerologist. But a numeroscope is based not only on a person's date of birth, but also a person's name — or names, as we will see.

The Birthdate
The birthdate is the universe's message to you, and that message is built, of course, on the day, month, and year of your birth. The first thing we do with a birthdate is total the numbers of the day, month, and year, and reduce the sum to one digit in the following way.

21 August 1925

$2 + 1 + 8 + 1 + 9 + 2 + 5 = 28$

$2 + 8 = 10$

$1 + 0 = 1$

So for this person, the universe is suggesting he learn the lessons of his Destiny Number 'one'.

The Destiny Number describes what you must learn about in your life time. You will continue to be put in situations that raise aspects of the Destiny Number until the lessons involved are learned. Then the opposite happens, and you get put into situations where those lessons help you and move you along to learning how much you can achieve. That's one of the reasons I put the meditation into the last chapter. It helps people pinpoint the lessons they have to learn this lifetime.

So, go back to the above example. This is a person who has to learn not to take others for granted, and not to see the world in terms of 'me first'. It is a person who must learn not to constantly compete with other people just to find out who is 'number one', especially when the question is academic. More than this, the Destiny Number is modified by the individual day, month, and year of birth. In other words, 21 August 1925 has a slightly different message from the universe than 12 August 1925 or 22 July 1952. The day, month, and year of birth are each called an 'aspect' of the Destiny Number.

The day of birth, or day aspect, provides details of what lessons must be learned in the person's day-to-day activities and in terms of family life and even internal life. Alternatively, it describes the joys available when the lessons have been learnt.

Bring it back to the above example of a person born on the twenty-first. This is a fairly fortuitous day to be born, indicating that the person will enjoy a fairly strong family life and always have a vivid imagination. But, the person will have to learn to express the deep emotions that arise. They will be someone who will begin life as a shy person, but will eventually overcome this by learning more and more to deal with other people on their terms without losing one's own frame of reference. This is a person who can easily take on the colour of events around them. This person must learn to do this without losing sight of their original intentions.

The month of birth, or month aspect, describes details of what a person must learn in their social, business, political, and community life. It can also show what successes a person might gain on the stage of life, if they would only try.

So, back to the example of somebody born in August. These people are those who are born to great success or great failure, depending on whether they learn to gauge others carefully and work within the limits of others. If they fail these lessons, then they will be spectacular failures. If they succeed, they can gain a niche for themselves in history.

The year of birth, or year aspect, gives us the details of a person's spiritual lessons. This is the most important of the three aspects, because it details the lessons of the Age the person lives in. To fail to learn the lessons is, in most cases, to fail the Destiny Number as well. To succeed is to have heaven and earth opened to you.

So what does 1925 mean? Start by totalling $1+9+2+5$ or 17;

$1 + 7 = 8$. So, just like the month, the year aspect is an eight. So it looks like the person's business, social, political, and community life is the most important aspect. It is likely, then, that the person is drawn to what they do by a calling. *Destiny* Number takes on a more rigid meaning, here.

But more than that, this person must learn not to be heavy or ponderous, but light, mobile, and able to keep an overview of the whole of matters in his or her own psyche.

Again, like the day aspect, people must be dealt with on their own terms. In terms of expressions, the way this person shows oneself to the world, this must be done in a lively manner; the person must be seen as expansive, generous, and keenly intellectual but also able to maintain artistic expression. The person must be seen as a humanitarian with an ability to perceive the true causes of things.

And finally, when building, the person must see details of what he or she is going to do. What processes will be involved, and what the general goal of life is.

Of course, when really examining the individual aspects, you would have to keep referring back to the original Destiny Number. So, the Destiny Number of six, to continue the example, would modify the year aspect. This is a person who must learn how to not have to be on top in each case, in every dispute. But equally, to be able to get the best out of others by judging how much they have to give (not how much they think they can give) and working with that, bringing them up to their maximum potential in life.

The Name
What's in a name? Well, details of your response to the universe's message to you, for one thing. It contains a description of your hopes, your drives, your fears, and probably how successful you will be in life.

The numerologist uses three versions of your name. Your Full Name uses the formal versions of all your names — first, middle, last, and if you have a confirmation name, both middle names. It doesn't include honorary titles like 'Sir', nor titles like 'Senior'. Just the names themselves are considered.

Your Formal Name is the name you use signing cheques, documents, in business, and so on. It can be one or two initials and your surname (e.g. M. A. Smythe) if that is how you sign things. However, in this case you do use titles like Sir, Lady, Junior, and so on if you use them as a matter of course.

Your Personal Name is the name people know you by. And if people know you by a nickname, that is the name you use. So if people call you Cleo, it doesn't matter if your name is really Cleopatra. If they call you Slim when your name is Harry, then Slim is your personal name.

Your Full Name is the primary response you give to the Destiny Number. In this, it also parallels the year aspect of your Destiny Number.

The Formal Name is your business, political, social and community way of looking at things. It parallels your month aspect most closely, though all names revert eventually to your Destiny Number.

Your Personal Name is the persona you use in your day-to-day and family affairs, and matches your day aspect and Destiny Number.

Now, this is not to say you have three personalities or you just put on different faces. Simply, people react differently in different situations. Too often we think the person is only as we see them; numerology realizes this is not the case.

So, when dealing with someone numerologically, use their full name as the primary basis of how hard or easy, or how successful or unsuccessful their lives will be. In this I include not only whether they get what they want, but whether their lives shall be lived in a way appropriate for them. In other words, there is in numerological thought a normative element. Part of the successful life is an 'ought'. Do they live as they ought to do, given their internal makeup, or will they try to change that to follow the whims of others? This is an important but ignored aspect of success.

The Formal and Personal names can modify your judgement of the Full Name, but in the main only in their areas of influence. So a well-aspected Formal Name will only aid in areas of business, social life, group life, politics, and so on. A well-aspected Personal Name will only help in friendship, love, day-to-day life, and so on.

'Aspected with what, and how?' is of course the next question.

In the main, it's aspected with the Destiny Number. If the Destiny

Number and the Full Name are compatible numbers, then the person's life will be relatively easy and the lessons of the universe will be learnt. If, however, they are incompatible, then the lessons will probably go unlearned, and the person will never attain the success they might otherwise have had.

If the Full Name and the Destiny Number are incompatible, but the Destiny Number and the Formal Name are compatible, then the person is likely to have business, social, political, cultural, and community success, but find that very success hollow. It's a common plot; the person who rises to the world stage while slowly making their personal life an absolute shambles.

If the Personal Name and Destiny Number are compatible, and the Destiny Number and Full Name aren't, then the person will have a happy personal life, but never one that amounts to much. Able to draw joy from a sunset or be ready with a good conversational joke, they will be unable to put things together in their lives, but will be buffeted along.

Mind you, the more aspects and Destiny Number that are compatible with names, the more successful the person will be in learning the lessons of the universe and in consequence the happier they will be in life.

We can summarize this in the chart below. The + 's refer to a name variation compatible with the Destiny Number, the − 's one that is incompatible. The columns are, from left to right, Full Name, Formal Name, and Personal Name. The column on the right summarizes the position the people are dealing with.

Fu.N.	F.N.	P.N.	
+	+	+	An ideal position where all lessons are learned, and life apparently idyllic. The Apollonius of Tyana position.
+	+	−	The politician style. Successful in every way where social strictures are involved, but some real and human element is missing. The Winston Churchill position.

Fu.N.	F.N.	P.N.	
+	–	+	Successful in minor things, or in helping others, but never able to put things together. Che Guevara position, or Trotsky.
–	+	+	Everything is tried, nearly successful, but then things start to slip away. Richard III. Does not get the major lessons in life.
+	–	–	A person unable to find a focus in life. Failures don't seem to teach them a better way of doing things. Tends to blame others for failure.
–	+	+	Successful in many ways, middle management type, but finding things hollow. Tends to boot lick.
–	+	–	Sacrifices everything for the image and quickly becomes one of life's voluntary victims.
–	–	+	Daily life is a respite only. The housefrau sort.
–	–	–	The person for whom nothing goes right. No lessons learned. Late, then becomes unlamented.

Head, Heart, and Hand Numbers

In addition to the three versions of your name, a numerologist looks at the vowels, consonants, and the totality of numbers as a separate element of the name. Each of these groupings tells us something different about you.

The vowels, by themselves, provide the Heart Number. This describes the person's inner desires, their secret wishes, and what they would like to be. If there is no other vowel, y is used as a vowel. In the Full Name, if the first, middle, or last name has only a y, then it is still used as a vowel even if there are vowels in the other two names.

The consonants alone give the Hand Number. This is what a person shows to the world, how he or she presents him or herself. It is the mask of the person, the persona they show to the world.

All the letters together give the Head Number. This is the totality of the person, and in particular, how they provide a reconciliation between the Heart and Hand Numbers.

The Head, Heart and Hand Numbers are not usually related back to the Destiny Number, and certainly not when you are just getting the feel of things. Instead, use them as amplifications of the numbers of the Full, Formal, and Personal Name numbers.

Take, for example, somebody whose Personal Name is Fred. This would give him a Heart Number of 5, a Hand Number of 19 or 1, and a Head Number of 6. If his Destiny Number were, say, 2, it would be compatible with the heart number, but neither the Head nor the Hand Number. In this we would look only at the Head Number, which is the whole of the Personal Name number. The compatibility with the Heart and Hand Numbers would not concern us.

What we would say about Fred is he is a person who secretly wants to be a wit, an intellectual, a person who has travelled. He presents himself to the world, in his day-to-day affairs, as pretty self-confident, and aware of who he is. But Fred's real concern is with responsibility and home life, and understanding others. We would say Fred has built a wall around himself and has been unable to tear it down. We say 'unable' because his Destiny Number is incompatible with his Personal Name Number, or Head Number.

Now, you've been hearing about compatible and incompatible numbers so much, you no doubt want to know what it all means, so that's next.

Compatibility

Just like music, where some notes are harmonious and others disharmonious, so in numerology some numbers work better together than others. Combinations of numbers can be confirming, extending, or disharmonious. The first two categories are compatible, the last incompatible. The system is shown below.

No.	Confirming	Extending	Disharmonious
1	4, 7	3, 8	2, 5, 6, 9
2	5, 8	4, 9	3, 6, 7, 1
3	6, 9	1, 5	4, 7, 8, 2
4	1, 7	2, 6	5, 8, 9, 3
5	2, 8	3, 7	6, 9, 1, 4
6	3, 9	4, 8	7, 1, 2, 5

No.	Confirming	Extending	Disharmonious
7	1, 4	5, 9	8, 2, 3, 6
8	2, 5	6, 1	9, 3, 4, 7
9	3, 6	7, 2	1, 4, 5, 8

A careful reading of the chart will show the easily-grasped principles involved. But to be complete, we should explain the system.

Start by putting the numbers 1 through 9 on a circle at even spaces, as shown in the illustration below.

Now, starting at 1, draw an equilateral triangle. You will find this touches 1, 4, and 7. Draw another triangle starting at 2, this touches 2, 5, and 8. A third will touch 3, 6, and 9. These triangles represent confirming numbers, and we show them below.

Again, starting with the circle of numbers, we can draw a nine-pointed star by connecting every second number. So, starting at 1, we move to 3, then 5, and so on around the circle, as shown below.

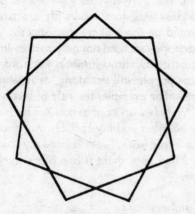

These are extending numbers. Any numbers not extending or confirming are considered disharmonious.

Confirming numbers indicate a relationship of mutual support and strengthening of attitudes. This doesn't mean the numbers are alike — the pioneer one, the steady four, and the reserved seven are all very different. It is more that each set of confirming numbers create a sort of 'working group'. People with one of these numbers dominant will work well with those with a confirming number. Each will add something to the relationship without trying to make the other change. Moreover, a full set of confirming numbers is necessary to complete any major project.

Extending numbers indicate a relationship where methods and ideas are put to the test, where a person is forced to grow. But that growth comes in a way that is developing and enjoyable. In this sort of relationship a person would be, say, made to play better and better opponents at chess. The object isn't to win more games, but to improve skills.

By contrast, in a confirming relationship, a person would play people of about the same level of competence but who have different styles of play. The object is for the person to be able to win more games.

Disharmonious numbers, on the other hand, challenge a person's way of life. This is not to say those ways might not prove themselves valid for a person, but only that they would be under challenge. However, it would be a long, hard road with no guarantee of success. Indeed, failure would be more likely than success.

These three categories are used not only to examine how a person's name numbers and their Destiny Numbers work out, but can be used for examining how people will get along, or how to enhance your chances for success. For example, the title of this book, *Numerology: The Power to Know Anybody* works out to be a 7. This is compatible with both my Destiny Number and my Full, Formal, and Personal Name Numbers. So with a little work, I've enhanced my chances of the book being published. Mind you, there is one other thing we work with in a numeroscope.

Counting the Numbers

Taking the letters of the Full Name, we count up how many of each digit we have. Take the following example.

Frederick Charles Whiteford

We then count out the numbers on the following chart.

No.	Examples
1	2
2	2
3	3
4	2
5	4
6	3
7	0
8	2
9	6

A surfeit of numbers — like the surfeit of sevens, will indicate especial areas of trouble. An overbalance of numbers will show areas of excesses. In this case, this person will have troubles being alone, and will have a tendency to excess in eating and aesthetic pleasures. This tool, however, is only a rough guide so that the aspect of the Destiny Number that will give the most trouble can be picked out. We will examine this in more detail in later chapters.

Summary

We are surrounded by numbers, not only our own but those of others. Our friends, our parents, our children, our workmates, everybody. More, the name of the company you work for (or are going to join), the political party you support, even the books you buy. These can all be understood by numbers.

With an understanding of what the universe is trying to tell you, and realizing what you've been saying back, you can establish better chances for yourself. You can not only know anybody else, you can know yourself. Once you do that, and numerology is an excellent way to do this, then great vistas of success and happiness, of right action and right thought, can be open to you. And that, really, is what we're about in this book.

CHAPTER THREE

THE MOST IMPORTANT CHAPTER IN THIS BOOK

Remember how in the introduction we spoke of the differences in the Pythagorean and Ulian systemata, and how the Ulian systemata does not reduce the value of a number down to a single digit? You may have wondered why it matters that A should be 1, J should be 10, and S be 100, rather than all three just being 1.

I think the best way to explain the difference is by example. Let's take somebody's full name, say it's

John Henry Hopkins

Using the Pythagorean systemata we would get the following from a numeroscope.

```
J o h n   H e n r y   H o p k i n s
1+6+8+5 + 8+5+5+9+7 + 8+6+7+2+9+5+1 = 92
9+2 = 11      1+1 = 2
```

So from this we could talk about him as diplomatic, patient, with a degree of wisdom, and so on. But take the same name with the Ulian systemata.

```
J o h n   H e n r y   H o p k i n s
10+60+8+50 + 8+5+50+90+700 + 8+60+70+20+9+50+100
= 1298
```

Now, while we can still use 2 as the general thrust of his name, we can also say each of the four numbers of '1298' means something on its own.

The number in the ones column is how a person is with him or her self. It's the number of a person's drive, ambition, what a person wants and reaches for. It is closest to the astrological sun-sign. In the case of John Henry Hopkins, then, we would have to say he is a person of great ambition, with a desire for organizational efficiency. The question at hand would be whether the other numbers back this up. Does he have the means to fulfil this desire?

The number in the tens column shows how a person deals with other people, how well a person uses diplomacy and tact, what wisdom he or she has and whether that wisdom is used. It is closest to the astrological moon-sign. In this case, we find Mr Hopkins deals with people by training them. He probably sees his chance in organizational strength in getting people to see things his way, and then dealing with them as equals. Clearly, people seem to be important to Mr Hopkins. We can also say Mr Hopkins has some wisdom, and lays great strength on whatever wisdom he may possess.

The number in the hundreds column represents a person's method of expression, how he or she presents him or herself to the world. It is good to remember, in this case, that a person's drive or wisdom may differ from how it is presented to the world. This is closest to the astrological rising sign. In the example, we find working with others and letting others benefit from his wisdom is how Mr Hopkins likes to express himself. We would expect him to have an amicable disposition, and a skill at expressing himself to people he knows.

The number in the thousands column — and remember there won't always be a number in this column — is the number of planning. It is the effect a person may have on history. Probably, these effects will be few, but what often seems of little effect will over time prove the key to understanding much. After all, history is made up of far more 'accidents' than we'd like to admit.

Most commonly, though, the number in the thousands column is simply how a person plans things out. How he or she organizes and builds, and leaves something to posterity. The most common number in this position is 1, and as per the example, it means the person just wants to leave behind something about him or herself. Mr Hopkins would want to leave something of himself behind in other people.

Possibly by having children but, thinking of the other three numbers in his full name, I'd say more likely he wants what he teaches to survive in other people.

The fifth number — this is rare — is a person as a representative of the species as a whole. It is his or her ability to grasp the principles along which humanity lives.

There are meanings to the other numbers as well, the hundreds of thousands column, millions, and so on. However, you'll never run across these unless you're doing an egregore (group soul) map. But that's well outside the scope of this book. For the most part, you will only ever be interested in the first three columns of a person's name.

Nevertheless, these last two chapters have given you the basic tools of a numerologist. What we will be doing next is showing you in detail how to use them.

CHAPTER FOUR

IT BEGINS AT BIRTH

In Chapter Two we had a brief look at the Destiny Number. This is the number imposed on you at birth, and which represents what the universe demands you learn in this lifetime. As we will see in the next chapter, it also provides cycles in which you learn these lessons. You see, everybody's life runs in cycles. The ancient Greeks, for example, saw it like this:

1st seven years the teeth grow in.
2nd seven years comes the ability to produce seed.
3rd seven years the beard grows and manhood is reached.
4th seven years, strength reaches maximum.
5th seven years is the season for marriage.
6th seven years the height of intelligence arrives.
7th seven years is the maturity of reason.
8th seven years is the perfection of intelligence and reason.
9th seven years is the period of equity and mildness, passions becoming gentle.
10th seven years is the end of desirable life.

Needless to say, numerologists have a more refined method now. Not only is the method more detailed, it includes girls as well as boys.

The Destiny Number
Your Destiny Number is the total of your date, month, and year of birth reduced to one digit. For example:

27 November 1923
$$2+7+1+1+1+9+2+3 = 26 \qquad 2+6 = 8$$

④

Thus 8 is the Destiny Number. But this can also be read in another way:

27	27	*28 = 1*
November	11	*7 = 7*
1923	1923	*1976 = 5*
	1961	*20 ? 1*

In other words, like the Ulian system in general, we can use the full Destiny Number to examine single aspects of your life's lesson. And we can take the individual date, month, or year of birth to analyse the aspects of the Destiny Number.

To get the most from your Destiny Number, begin by totalling your birthdate as shown, and reducing the whole to one digit. This is the most important number, and it will guide all others in what you must learn. Then turn to each of the aspects. The day of birth will tell you what you have to learn in your day-to-day affairs. Your month of birth outlines what you must understand in your business and social affairs. The year of birth provides the spiritual lesson you must learn.

Finally, the full number of your destiny, in the example above, 1961. The first digit will show you how you must learn to see yourself. The tens digit will tell you how you must learn to deal with others. The number in the hundreds column is how you must learn to present yourself to the world, the form rather than the content of your message. The number in the thousands column is the number of planning and this is always one, at least in Western society.

When you have done that, turn to the guide below to learn what you have to learn, and what success in that will mean.

1.

Your major lesson in life is to understand that the sun doesn't rise and set on you. It's going that way and you just get in the way. One's have to learn they are not always at the centre of things. Others get to have their day in the sun, too.

This is part-in-parcel with your spiritual lesson. You must learn a temperate balance in your emotions and interests. Like the sun you can provide life-giving warmth, but you can also wither with your glare or turn cold and withdraw from others. To overcome this, you must learn to do things in natural cycles. You have to learn the value of temperance.

Take a typical case, where the worst sort of one runs roughshod over others, and then loses faith in him or herself when the crunch comes. Only then does he or she think, 'Perhaps I should have listened to . . .', but by then it's too late. It would have been easier to take advice in the beginning, but realize in the end all life is a bet on yourself.

Benefit from this by being less anxious in day-to-day life. Neither blow little things out of proportion nor ignore them as ephemeral. If you spend a little forethought, many of those problems of daily life will disappear.

You are naturally a pioneer and this factor helps you greatly. It would be to your advantage to see yourself as an explorer of new territories of time. Whether in business or social meetings or dealing with people, or just waking up to face a new day, see each situation as something fresh and new. However, if you haven't learned temperance and patience, this exercise can back-fire, so learn those two lessons first.

To learn these two virtues, try to see yourself not as an individual but as a condensation of your environment. Just as your patron star, the Sun, seems all conquering but is in fact only one of a galaxy of stars, so you are a part of humanity.

Try presenting yourself in this way. Remember that those who are most brash and seemingly most confident are the ones who are the least secure. They are the ones who fail at crucial moments in their lives. If you learn this you will find the key to an Alladin's cave of new ideas, creative thought, happy activity and joyful life. Fail and you will be put in exactly the same position you were before.

In brief: Learn about your limits, take others into account, patience, humility, temperance. You are one of many and the many join together. Expect joy but don't demand it, it will come when the time is right.

2.

In business and society you have to learn to stick up for yourself, and in your spiritual and day-to-day concerns you must learn to separate fact from fantasy. These may seem disparate requirements, but they are closely connected. Simply because others want something doesn't mean you have to give it to them, nor do you have to agree with prevailing opinions to 'keep the peace'.

Like your Earth-mother patron planet, you want to nurture things. You want to give of yourself to others. This is all well and good, but remember that if you over crop a field, the Earth-mother rebels. She allows enough, but never too much. So while it might be nice to fantasize about endless plenty, separate fact from fancy and remember there are no free lunches.

This means that there must be some sort of line drawn between acceptable and excessive. This line is your own principles judging the real facts of the case. If you allow fantasy and fact to mix, you will never have a reliable measure by which to judge that line. If you fail in this, your diplomacy and tact will degenerate into hypocrisy and boot-licking. There are times when you will have to deal with others from the shoulder and accept the confrontation that may expose — not cause, but only expose.

You should see yourself as a well from which others drink. Don't think only of the fountainhead of the well, though, remember the whole image of the well. Every well needs an underground stream to feed it, and a natural filter to purify the water if it is to be any good for the people and animals who will drink from the well. So while a well may seem inexhaustible, it must be used sparingly. Block off the waters, take away the purifier, or just use the well too much and the well will no longer be useful.

You must always be certain of your access to your source of things. However much life may try to break these links, you must hold them secure. Without this, people will be no more than vultures seeking your time, space, and money. This is your overall lesson in life.

Only by strengthening those links will you be able to judge fact from fantasy. Then and only then will you be able to separate the genuine from the fake, those who are honest from those who are throwing you a line. You will find this invaluable in your business and social lives, and it should be the cornerstone of all activities in these fields.

Strong links with your source, however you define that source, is also the key to how you should present yourself to others. Preserve the quiet dignity of the Earth-mother who is diplomat and nurturer, but who also judges her children and shows when she finds them wanting.

In brief: Learn your strengths and hold to them, pursue the quiet dignity of being secure in your thoughts and opinions and turn aside those who demand you change your ways as if this validates their opinions, be ruthless with the urge to cloud fact with fantasy, learn the virtue of determination.

3.

In day-to-day life you live a happy-go-lucky style that suits you but which, if you are not careful, will make you a well known nuisance. You will have to realize others may not find you being constantly late all that enervating. It is fortunate for you that your creativity and a greater willingness to organize yourself keeps your business and formal social life on a more even keel.

It would be wise to remember Jupiter wasn't only the jovial seducer, but as Jupiter Optimus Maximus he was the god of cosmic justice, patron of the Roman Senate, and he was the awesome thunderer. These were responsible positions and you should learn about them or you will be in danger of becoming the perpetual Peter Pan. You would do well to see yourself in each of the roles fulfilled by your patron planet, not just the one. At least, do so some of the time, if not at all times.

Your spiritual lesson is to learn the origin, nature, and uses of the twin forces of enthusiasm and creativity. The enthusiasm we are talking about is a divine inspiration that sweeps you off your feet and puts you almost into a trance. This, too, was a function of Jupiter.

If you learn about these forces, you will no longer depend on luck, you will know what your luck really is. It will put an end to some aspects of your happy-go-lucky style, but only because you will now no longer accept luck as a 'gift from the gods' but will in many circumstances be able to control it not only for yourself but for those around you. In this sense, learning about enthusiasm is something of a means to an end. It not only is part of your luck, but a factor in your creativity.

It is only through your creativity that you will learn concern for others. It isn't the source of that concern, but the key to opening that particular door in your life. That in turn will lead you to become a more reliable person, and reliability is the task you must master as your overall lesson in this lifetime.

By 'reliable' I don't mean staid or boring or taking a certain line. I mean keeping promises, respecting other peoples' enthusiasms. I mean learning to be honest rather than merely blunt, and learning to present yourself to others with honesty and consideration. If you can do this, your life will be lived to the full and you will enjoy all of it.

In brief: Be creative but learn from the sensibilities of others, pursue the origin of your enthusiasm and creativity and base your life's work on that, develop a sense of responsibility.

4.

There are two sorts of fours in the world, those who organize and those who are more zealous of the law than they are of its followers. Get in column A and stay there: that is your overall lesson in life. The latter type of four frequently becomes a dullard who sees every change as a direct and personal threat and who always says everything was better 'back then'.

This doesn't mean you need to go in for wholesale change or massive reforms. Your spiritual lesson in the world is to uphold a rigid measuring stick. After all, your patron planet is Saturn, and in ancient times it marked the known boundary of the solar system. It was the planet of tests, trials, and age. But Saturn was not seen (by experts) as a harsh master, for he was also a preserver who helped sort good from bad. To do this, his measuring rod was used.

The secret of preserving standards is to preserve the process rather than the result, and the intent of the law rather than its letter. For example, it is more important that an election be fair than who wins.

Again, it is more important that individuals preserve piety than the rites be letter perfect. In the same way, in your business and social life it is important that you remain 'on square' and remember 'rectitude' means 'right angled'. That is, maintain honesty and discipline in your dealings with others.

This is important to your organizational skills. To you, system is not simply a system of rules but is a fairer means of doing things because, at its best, it deals with all people equally. This, to you, is far better than having a person, or luck, make the decision on a whim. This reflects well on your business and social life, but you would do well to remember to present yourself to others not simply as organized, but to show rectitude is the basis of your concern for organization.

You must see yourself as one who 'follows the correct path' and meets others along the way. If you do this, it will serve your dealings with others well. You must always maintain that single measuring rod against which to measure yourself and others. But don't use this as an excuse to become too strict. Your zealousness, remember, must be for the followers, not the law. It's still okay to have fun, to loosen up. Standards can be kept without being inflexible.

In brief: Maintain standards of process, reject what isn't good, follow the path of rectitude, a standard all can match is best, make use of your organizational skills, be more zealous of followers than of the law.

5.

You have to learn not to leap on every passing fancy, but to tie your enthusiasm to a single star and ride it to the four winds of the universe. This is your spiritual lesson in life. Too often fives take in influences at random and achieve nothing that lasts. Your overall lesson, then, is to learn to be able to look inwards, to be able to look and really see the world.

Remember the Age of Pisces was a five age; the five elements (spirit, air, fire, water, and earth) corresponding to the five messiahs (Lao Tzu, Buddha, Jesus, Mohammed, and Marx, respectively). You must see yourself as leaving behind the strife, evils and conflicts of the Piscean Age.

To do this, you must overcome the fact that this is the time when you are most in danger of dissipation. You must guide your day-to-day life by maintaining inner discipline. This, in turn, means concentrating your energies and setting some things as being out of bounds for you. You can't be a master of all trades and you can't be successful in all the areas that interest you.

The same rule applies to your business life. Don't try to do a bit of everything, this may be the trend in business now, but so are falling profits and the abuse of employees, and the trends are related. Mercury is your patron planet, so remember he wasn't just a traveller and a quick thinker, he was also a thief and a liar. So, instead of dissipating your energies, take one or two specialities and relate everything back to them. You will be amazed at the effects, not only in business and social life, but in your day-to-day life as well. You will find people will listen to what you have to say more often, because what you say will be more likely to be right, more considered. Yet, you will find you have as much freedom as you ever had, and your life will be filled with more fascinating events, people and ideas than you ever dreamed possible.

You should present yourself in life as a person with a lively interest in life itself, rather than a wastrel who will listen to anything for a little while, or try anything once, and then drop it. If you don't believe in the effectiveness of this, try going to four parties and discuss nothing about yourself but what you have actually achieved. Remember that people expect a certain degree of constancy from other people, or at least those they care about. If you cannot actually be consistent, at least let people know where the transitions are.

It is said there are too many specialists and not enough generalists. It would be truer to say there are too many specialists who don't have a range of interests outside their field of speciality. Your destiny is to work towards being a specialist interested in all life. You may sample exotic fruits, but you will have to learn to make practical use of them.

In brief: Don't follow fads, have a speciality or two illumed by a wide range of interests, you must wrap up the Piscean Age, learn about your internal life and the origin of your thoughts and learn to control and use them to affect the outer world.

6.

Your spiritual lesson is to learn about responsibility and harmony in the widest senses of these words. This means not only to take responsibility but also to understand what it really is and to be able to apportion it. You must learn why harmony exists and how to promote it. These two tasks mean you must see yourself as balancing the forces of harmony and responsibility against each other, and learn to understand they sometimes aid and sometimes hinder each other.

This can make your dealings with other people seem complicated, since the two urges will so often be in conflict with each other. Equally, this is what some say is the meaning of the uniscursial hexagram illustrated in Chapter 1. In this view, it shows two forces arising from a common origin, contending for a time, and then remerging or resolving at a higher level of existence. The secret during all of this (and this is your overall lesson for this life) is to keep things in balance during this process. Thus there is enough harmony so responsibility is accepted, enough responsibility to preserve harmony, all in due measure.

Your business affairs and social life can gain from this, of course, but there is a greater benefit to be had from the forces of your patron planet, the Moon. Remember that to the ancients the Moon was a mysterious and changeable object. It detailed the weekly cycle by its phases and, when the period of those phases grouped together was used, the monthly cycle. It was therefore a timepiece of a regular, cyclical event, and though many choose to forget the fact, business and social concerns run in cycles. Like the Moon, business and society waxes and wains and you have to learn to work within these various cycles.

The same applies to your day-to-day life. Learn which of your days are waxing days and which are waning days and operate appropriately. Do the heavy tasks on waxing days, while on waning days do those small tasks of review or tying up loose ends. Begin all your important projects on the gibbous or full Moon. Start nothing of import on the new Moon, but use that time to close off projects, throw things out, and so on.

Interlace this lunar cycle with the cycles of destiny described in the next chapter to provide a fairly comprehensive schedule of what to do with your days.

When you are presenting yourself to other people, consider yourself a person who understands and utilizes harmony and responsibility. Others may be put off by someone who changes demeanour every week, but don't forget your patron planet is the Moon, ruled by Hecate, and she was a triple goddess. She was virgin, mother and hag, and growth, exaltation, and vengeance. So where you should be constant in your goals, your hopes, and your spiritual drive, vary your method of handling things.

In brief: Keynote responsibility and harmony and their interactions, learn their common origin, learn the value of cyclical activity and how to use cycles to make your every action and thought more effective.

7.

Both your spiritual and overall lesson in life is to understand how spirit creates, shapes, and controls matter. This means the hubbub and bustle of daily life is not the stuff of what you require for proper life. Instead, you are to live as a contemplator, standing one step removed from modern life and learning to understand the fundamental laws of nature.

However, the pace of modern life, especially for those of us with jobs, families, and television sets, is seductive. To keep yourself on track, take some time out and ask yourself some questions:

1. Where do I really want to go in life?
2. What do I really want to do with my time?
3. Where do I want to be five years from now?
4. What can I do to improve my life?

You have to wrestle hard with each of these questions, and you have to be willing to add others to the list. It's useless taking the quick and easy answers. If you put down what others want you to want, you will only be reinforcing that very hubbub you were trying to purge yourself of in the first place. There is no prisoner more trapped than one who refuses to escape.

But just because you avoid the hubbub of life does not mean you have to pull out of any business or social life. You can be the linchpin drawing together those subtle influences that make both yourself and others grow. If you fail in this, unmitigated disaster follows. You must remember to operate from internal strength and eternal principles.

In dealing with others, this means having to consider the long-term. Avoid the expediency of the moment, even if it does cause you some stress at times. Stop-gap measures never solve the problem.

Like your patron planet, Venus, you must remain removed from the world so that you can be an objective observer. If, for example, you accept the power of an external hierarchy rather than work from your inner strength, then that hierarchy has captured you, and you can no longer be an observer.

This distance between you and the world is what allows you access to the universal storehouse of ideas. If you lose that grip on the divine, you will never complete your tasks in life. Preserve the link, and never compromise it or use it for shallow purposes. In this context, answer the great questions of life first, and you will find the minor questions will answer themselves.

In brief: Contemplate life, meditate on imponderables, preserve integrity at all costs, understand universal laws, observe things carefully and relate them to those universal laws, preserve your link with the divine.

8.

Your overall lesson is to develop your sense of justice, and use that sense to guide your use of the other forces which you can tap. You must realize you have the power to give concrete form to the lofty ideals of, say, the sevens of the world. To many this might seem a strange role for someone whose patron planet is Pluto, but remember Pluto wasn't only the god of the dead but also of the wealth that could be gained from the ground. With his brothers Neptune and Jupiter, he was one of the ruling triumvirate of the gods.

Like Pluto, you follow a path of commerce and power and organization. However, your spiritual lesson is to maintain the value of the ideal over that of the pragmatic.

One example of this lies in dealing with other people. You can be in danger of promoting conformity to the status of a virtue. Try to remember if other people follow a different path, it doesn't mean they are wrong, just that they are going to some other place. Learn to deal with others on the basis of mutual respect and believe that everyone is a person in their own right. If you don't, you will invariably be trying to control others and they will turn on you for this.

Your day-to-day life as well as your business and social life must be guided by a principle so old as to have become almost forgotten. It's so old that the best English word for it is 'interlockingness'. It's the belief that everything is connected to everything else.

In a small way the principle is used in ecology and economics, but these are fairly specialized fields. Remember, in your own use of this principle, that your thoughts and actions are connected to the universe. What you do invariably affects the world, and anything done in the world affects you. With your thoughts alone, you can make the world a better place.

Remember the ogdoad was always a symbol of the divine: the Knights Templar wore an eight-rayed star on their tunics, Egyptians associated it with Osiris returning to the primal source of being. Note here, Osiris, like Pluto, was a god of the dead and a god of wealth. It would be wrong for you to misuse your power, and so you must see yourself as bringing the inner strength of justice to all you do.

Your destiny compels you to discover the links of things, those aspects of life that are examples of the 'interlockingness' of the universe. You must learn what these links mean. How does spirit interact with matter, organizer with organization, sea with land? All these things have their linkage, a point that is neither one nor the other, but a place of transition. It is being able to understand that this makes you realize conformity is not a virtue. It's also vital if you are going to bring the lofty ideals into practice in the everyday world — there is, after all, a link between could be and is.

Yours is often quoted as a number of extremes, but this should be expected from a number of great power and opportunity.

In brief: Beware your own power, seek the links of change, the interlockingness of the world, preserve the powers of justice as the guiding light of your organizational skills, make the lofty ideals of others concrete, you have the power to reify by action.

9.

You have two patron planets, Mars and Neptune. Remember that most initiation rites are based on the premise of divulged secrets being provided if and only if certain tests or challenges are passed successfully. Mars is the test and Neptune represents the secrets. If you have grasped this, you pretty well have the secret of your spiritual lesson in life. And if you can apply it to your every waking thought, then you have the secret of applying your spiritual lesson to your day-to-day life.

To achieve this knowledge and its application, two things must happen. You must overcome a love of the 'glorious I' which so many nines fall prey to, and you must grasp the broad principles of human life. It is your overall lesson to make generosity, love, and humanitarianism second nature to you. Here, as in so many things in life, an overstuffed ego is prequel to disaster, and only by looking at the broad scope will the ego get unstuffed and the path of initiation be found.

Initiation is the path, but it is the beginning, middle, and end of the path; it is the goal and the entrance, the spark and outcome. You will not necessarily become an initiate of one of the six occult paths, but you will become aware of the powers outside your conscious mind. We are, after all, at the changing of the Ages and subtle forces are coming to the fore.

You will have to learn to use these same forces in business and social life. Trust your intuition, your first reaction to things. Gauge them by how you see yourself; as student and teacher at once. What can you learn from people, what can you teach them? This will tell you how important someone can be to you.

See yourself, and just as importantly present yourself as a way-shower Not someone who says, 'This is right' but someone who leads by understanding. Moreover, someone who realizes that just because one person has gone through the barriers of initiation doesn't mean others won't benefit by learning the same things for themselves. Remember, when the Order initiates someone, it doesn't say, 'Oh, you can't have that test, we gave it to someone else.'

This is part of your spiritual lesson. Accept that other people have to pass their tests to gain their own access to the mysteries of life. In the same way, if you want to gain the secret, don't expect someone who is already there to be able to part the veil before you pass the tests. This is the secret of eliminating the ego of the 'glorious I'.

In brief: Be a way-shower to yourself, and realize everybody has to tread the path for themselves, beware of the 'glorious I' that wants kudos for things not yet done, grasp the broad humanitarian principles, be concerned for others.

CHAPTER FIVE

THE CYCLES OF DESTINY

Like your date of birth, every day of your life is stamped with numerological significance. This is true of every culture, for every culture creates and shapes its calendar along the needs and guy-lines it expresses. It does this in exactly the same way it develops its language and alphabet to express numerological principles. What I will say here, then, applies to any calendar you normally use, whether Jewish, Arabic, Chinese, Julian, or any of the esoteric calendars. The figures I will use, however, are from the standard Julian calendar.

In personal use, there are three major cycles which we normally use, the daily, the monthly, and the yearly. So, as an example, what sort of cycles would a person face on 12 October 1987 if he were born on 13 January 1956?

The calculations are the easy part. Start with the birthdate and substitute that part of the new date the cycle of which you want to determine. So, to use the example, the day cycle is calculated:

$$
\begin{array}{ll}
12 & 12 \\
\text{January} & 01 \\
1956 & 1956 \\
& 1969 \qquad 1+9+6+9=25 \qquad 2+5=7
\end{array}
$$

In other words, we just replaced 13, the birthdate, with 12, the date of the day we were concerned about. However, if we are reducing to one digit, every 12th of every month will come out a seven day.

To get the cycle of the month, we do much the same thing:

13	13
October	10
1956	1956
	1979 $1 + 9 + 7 + 9 = 26$ $2 + 6 = 8$

And the same process for the year cycle:

13	13
January	01
1987	1987
	2001 $2 + 1 = 3$

These are the bare bones of calculation. The important part is figuring out what they mean.

At the simpler level, check whether the cycle number is harmonious or disharmonious to the aspect of the Destiny Number, or to the Destiny Number itself. In the above example, we would look at it this way:

The day aspect of the Destiny Number is just the date of birth, in this case 13 or 4. The day cycle is 7, a confirming number. We would then be likely to say that if this person is learning the lessons the universe has set for this lifetime, it will be a good day. If not, it will be a bad day. In the same way, we would have a look at the month and year cycles.

We would also have a look at the Destiny Number itself. In this case, it is 8. The Destiny Number and the day cycle are disharmonious. We would have to say then that, while it is likely to be a good day (4 aspect and 7 cycle), no lasting effects are likely to come of it (8 Destiny Number and 7 cycle).

When doing this sort of rule of thumb analysis, there are actually four sorts of relationships we use, two harmonious and two disharmonious. These relationships are the Exaltation or Confirming; Strength or Extending; Detriment or Trial; and Fall or Impediment.

Exaltation: Confirming Numbers
Confirming numbers indicate a time of support and strengthening of attitudes. When cycles are confirming to the Destiny Number or

appropriate aspect, you will find things going your way. This doesn't mean you get your own way, for there is such a thing as a blessing in disguise, and on these days you will find even when things seem to be going badly, they will work out as being the best possible thing that could have happened to you. The more confirming relationships in the cycles, the more you are going to find you are succeeding in all your activities.

Strength: Extending Numbers

If these numbers influence your cycles, you will find yourself being put to the test. You will find yourself growing and developing, your karmic lessons being tucked under your belt and karmic debts falling by the wayside. It won't be easy, it will be a hard-fought satisfaction. However, projects and hopes are not usually realized in this relationship between cycles and Destiny. This is a time of progress, but not final triumph.

Detriment: Trial Numbers

These are periods where there may be many blind alleys for you. Avenues you have counted on will fall away, and you will have to decide whether to try to crash through or to seek another path. It's when your cycles and Destiny are in this sort of relationship you ought to trim your sales and off-load deadweight in your life. This is when the universe will most thoroughly remind you about those aspects of its lesson you have yet to learn.

Fall: Impediment Numbers

When the cycle and Destiny disagree to this extent, it's likely to be a time when absolutely nothing seems to go right. This is not just a test, it is more of an imperious command that you had better mend your ways or else. Where in Trial numbers you might be going the wrong way with good intentions, here you are simply blowing it, and should expect disaster. Mind you, if you are refusing all the lessons, even confirming days will turn out bad. If you are going through all the lessons, even impediment days will see good things happen.

To sum up the relationships. Confirming numbers are likely to produce results, things will come to fruition, and work will go smoothly.

Extending numbers still produce development, but also demand hard work from you. There is less likelihood of conclusion, more of progress. Trial numbers see hazards and failures which can be used to rebuild and grow. Impediment numbers are likely to see collapse, when you will feel like you are bashing your head against a wall. Confirming and Extending we see as 'good', Trial and Impediment as 'bad'.

However, we can be more explicit than this. If we go back to our earlier example, we can draw a partial numeroscope of the Destiny Number, its aspects, and the cycles.

	Destiny Number	
	8	
Aspect	Day	Cycle
4		7
Aspect	Month	Cycle
1		8
Aspect	Year	Cycle
3		3

Basically, the eight Destiny Number is repeated in the month cycle, so that would indicate something very important in this person's business or social life is about to happen. Since the aspect of the month is 1, and 1 is an Extending number of eight, it is likely to be a trying but successful time. However, the problem of ego is likely to rise. Because both one and eight use intuition in a particular way, this person will probably stumble on a good idea which can't be 'proved' beforehand. There will probably be some leap in career, for example, starting a new business or joining a new company. The test is whether this person will trust instincts or demand an impossible proof.

However, the year aspect and cycle is three. This reinforces a significant period, but does not bode well for success. Three is a Trial number of eight. That means the universe is trying to tell this person to back off on some way of doing things. The day aspect and cycle, however, are mutually Confirming numbers, so in day-to-day life there is a pretty good day going here. However, 4 is Trial number to eight, and 7 is Impediment, so there is little likelihood of that joy spilling over into the business life.

So if things are likely to go wrong, can they be put right? This is one of the advantages of numerology, because forewarned is forearmed. Remember from the last chapter that anybody with an eight Destiny Number should learn the principle of interlockingness to gain a guide to proper social and business life. This is the principle that would have to be emphasized. It is the solution of the problem. Now look at the reading for the Destiny Number of one, and look for the weakness.

It isn't hard to find. Learn to be temperate and let others have their day in the sun. This is not far from the eight weakness of raising conformity to a virtue. Both show a danger of running roughshod over others and then losing faith in themselves in a crunch.

The solution is then to tell this person to listen to others, take everything into account, make his or her decision by following intuition, and then jumping without looking back. Then the trial of the year will come out successfully. In this way an individual can gain insight into the lessons of the universe, use them, and gain thereby.

It should also be pointed out that, especially when your Destiny Number pops up in cycles, it often means you can get a thread of destiny. If you have never experienced it, no description will suffice. Let it just be described as a 'rush of knowledge and action'. You know what will happen, you can bend things to your will, you can feel palpable energy in your veins, and you can run yourself straight into a metaphysical wall. You may have the threads of destiny, you never see the whole tapestry. However exciting it is, watch yourself.

I should also point out that the description of cycles and aspects given above is pretty general. For a complete description we would need the name of this person as well. The schedule of the relations of numbers, though, will give you a good guide to what sort of day you will have on any date in your life. It goes like this.

Relationship of Numbers

No.	Confirming	Extending	Trial	Impediment
1	4, 7	3, 8	5, 6	2, 9
2	5, 8	4, 9	6, 7	1, 3
3	6, 9	1, 5	7, 8	2, 4

No.	Confirming	Extending	Trial	Impediment
4	1, 7	2, 6	8, 9	3, 4
5	2, 8	3, 7	1, 9	4, 6
6	3, 9	4, 8	1, 2	5, 7
7	1, 4	5, 9	2, 3	6, 8
8	2, 5	6, 1	3, 4	7, 9
9	3, 6	7, 2	4, 5	1, 8

As in Chapter 2, the geometric principles behind this list are very simple. To illustrate them, there are four illustrations below, one for each of the relationships. Trial numbers derive from one form of enneagram, Extending numbers from another form of enneagram. Impediment numbers are those next to the original numbers, and Extending numbers are those of three interlacing triangles.

Confirming

Extending

Trial

Impediment

To get the complete picture of cycles, you should also know something about how your Name Number can strengthen or weaken those cycles. Simply learn if your Full Name Number and your Destiny Number are Impediments, Trials, Extensions, or Confirmations. Then:

If your name number *Confirms* your Destiny Number then strengthen Confirming and Extending cycles and weaken your Trial and Impediment cycles. Equally, you probably won't achieve great things in life.

If your name number *Extends* your Destiny Number then strengthen your Extending and Trial cycles and weaken your Confirming and Impediment cycles. Great things may be possible, but the road will be tough.

If your name number *Tries* your Destiny Number, then strengthen your Confirming and Impediment cycles and weaken your Extending and Trial cycles. A pretty ordinary life in most ways, may be a roller coaster of highs and lows.

If your name number *Impedes* your Destiny Number, then strengthen your Trial and Impediment cycles and weaken your Confirming and Extending cycles. You have turned your back on what the universe has sought to teach you.

If a particular cycle is strengthened, then its influences will be more pronounced, and to a trained eye more visible. Where weakened, a cycle takes on less bite, performs fewer tasks, and is sometimes all but shunted aside.

Such are the basic rules of the cycles of destiny. However, numerology depends as much on the person's name as their birthdate, and it's the name we look at next.

CHAPTER SIX

NAME ANALYSIS: PART ONE

Your name is a vital part of the description of your soul. It is vital not only in describing where your soul is, but where it wants to go; its hopes and fears, how you present yourself to the world, how you deal with other people, and even the secret plans you have laid. Each of these things is described in one or another variant of your own name.

There are, after all, two methods of looking at your name; look at the variants of the name, and the different letters in your name. In this chapter, we will look at the former criterion. We will be looking at your Full, Formal, and Personal Names.

Full Name

Your Full Name is your first, middle, and last names, including both your middle names if you have two. However, it does not include titles like Sir or Lady or Jnr or Snr, or the maiden name of a married woman if she hasn't kept use of her maiden name. You should also be sure to use the full version of the names included, for example, it's always Benjamin in a Full Name, never Ben.

Your Full Name reveals the totality of you and what you will strive to become in the long term.

Formal Name

Your Formal Name is the name you use when signing cheques, business letters, forms, contracts, and so on. For example, if you use two initials and a surname, this would be your Formal Name. Your Formal Name also includes any titles you normally use in your signature, so your Formal Name could be B. M. Farnham or Lady Stockton.

This is the name that reveals your business and social affairs, and for many people it also guides their political aspirations as well.

Personal Name

Your Personal Name is what your friends and relatives call you, and this includes nicknames. So if your name is Fred but everybody calls you Junior, then Junior is your Personal Name. This holds true for shortened versions of names, for example, if you are called Mal, then that and not Malcolm is your Personal Name.

Your Personal Name describes your day-to-day life.

Where someone changes his or her name in life, whether through marriage, adoption, deed poll, or whatever, use the new name, not the old. However, expect a 'gap' of between three weeks and three months before the new name becomes an accurate description of the person. This same process applies to changing the spelling of a name.

Before, when I described the difference between the Ulian systemata and the Pythagorean systemata, I showed how a name like John Henry Hopkins could be analysed, not only by the single digit number of the Pythagorean systemata, but the extended number of the Ulian systemata. The same holds true if you use different variants of the same name. So, let's take the example, and say he signs his cheques John Hopkins and that, quite reasonably, his friends call him John. Under the Ulian systemata we get:

Full Name

J o h n   H e n r y   H o p k i n s
$10 + 60 + 8 + 50 + 8 + 5 + 50 + 90 + 700 + 8 + 60 + 70 + 20 + 9 + 50 + 100$
$= 1298$
$1 + 2 + 9 + 8 = 20$ $2 + 0 = 2$

Formal Name

J o h n   H o p k i n s
$10 + 60 + 8 + 50 + 8 + 60 + 70 + 20 + 9 + 50 + 100 = 445$
$4 + 4 + 5 = 13$ $1 + 3 = 4$

Personal Name
 J o h n
$10 + 60 + 8 + 50 \qquad = 128$
$1 + 2 + 8 = 11 \qquad 1 + 1 = 2$

From this thumbnail sketch we can determine a fair amount of Mr Hopkins' attitude to life and himself. To do so, we have to analyse this part of the numeroscope bit by bit, knowing how to flow along with the information provided.

Notice, for example, how his Full and Personal Names have the same basic number and quite similar extended numbers. We can say Mr Hopkins is probably fairly happy with his life and himself. His business life, guided by his Formal Name, has a basic number which is extending to his other name numbers, and this probably means he finds business and social life challenging, stimulating, sometimes frustrating, and often exhausting. So, given a suitable Destiny Number and its aspects, Mr Hopkins has every chance of a rather fulfilling life at whatever level of society he lives.

But if we use the extended numbers, we can elaborate on this. Start with the Full Name's 1298. As the basic number 2, we can see Mr Hopkins works with a hope of some modicum of wisdom and tries to be fairly adaptable. Probably there is some ideal image of the home that fuels Mr Hopkins' dreams.

His image of himself in this regard is as a man who is fairly well organized, with an ability to lead others. He has a concept of himself as a strong and just man, and probably sees parentage resting on a cornerstone of justice. We can tell this from the 8 in the ones column of his Personal and, secondarily, Full Names.

One quickly gets the impression Mr Hopkins divides himself between personal and business life. Though he may find the two complimentary, he probably keeps them separate.

Examine how he deals with other people, taking the three numbers in the tens column. Overall he is inclined to be generous, liberal, and humanitarian, as seen by the 9 in his Full Name. This is reinforced by the 2 in his Personal Name, which emphasizes tact and diplomacy. He is a person who, since 9 is extending to 2, is likely to try to get the best from people. Yet in his business and social lives we have a 4, showing a stricter person with a greater belief in organization, a person rather less creative than the Full Name 9 might suggest.

This belief in organization, though, continues when we look at the hundreds column in the Formal Name; here, too, is a 4. What we have here is an 'up front' sort who says he wants to see everyone working hard and follows hard by working hard, himself. This is interesting in the light of the 5 in the ones column of the Formal Name, which indicates a self-image of a quick-witted and friendly person.

Since 4 and 5 are impediments we would guess what Mr Hopkins tries to say and what he gets across are often very different things. At this point we are only guessing, but it's possible he would be inclined to believe friendliness will come 'when the work is finished' or some other condition that cannot be fulfilled.

Overall, however, his self-expression is based on the 2 in the hundreds column of the Full Name, and this is reinforced by the 2 basic number of the Full and Personal Names. He seeks to be tactful, diplomatic, and forthright, to be patient and loyal, and succeeds in this. In his personal life the hundreds column of his Personal Name number shows he expresses himself in an energetic sort of way. This combination shows he likes physical activity and probably abhors a night alone when there are discos or sports or some such to go to, and that probably (almost definitely) with friends.

This would seem to provide us a clue to his adaptable aspects. He likes to be with groups of people and will adapt plans to fit in with those of the 'group'.

We could go on from here, but you no doubt see the various ramifications of using the Full, Formal, and Personal Names coupled with the Ulian systemata. To gain any real mastery of the method, you have to practice on one numeroscope after another. This means using friends, neighbours, strangers, media figures and anybody else you can think of. Fortunately, most people are rather happy guinea pigs even when you get it wrong.

And, if you are already familiar with another school of numerology, then the name varients of the Ulian systemata and extended numbers can be transferred to that school independently.

But, to return to our methods, remember that it isn't only proper names that can be analysed. The same techniques can be used to investigate a business, organization, club, church, government department, political party and even country. The one real variable to worry about is the 'optional' parts of a company's name.

Greek numerologists would sometimes use the definite article as part of a word when deriving its meaning. In our terms, 'the chair' would be used to discern the meaning of 'chair'. This wasn't done in all cases. In dealing with companies we have a similar problem in whether to use 'the', 'PLC', 'Ltd', 'Inc', and so on as part of the company's name for the numeroscope. There is no simple answer of when to include these elements and when not to. Some companies take Ltd as an integral part of their names and some use it for purely legal reasons. I have found only three clues to whether to include these additional elements.

1. On letterheads and similar advices, is 'Ltd' and other titles included at the same size as the other words in the name of the company? If so, it's probably to be used in the numeroscope of its name. If smaller, it's more likely to be dropped.
2. Is the word 'the' included in posters and logos? If so, include it in the numeroscope.
3. Work backwards part of the way. Find out what you can about a group, fix what should be in part of the numeroscope by observation. Then test out names and see which fits observed details and the rest should follow.

An imperfect system, I admit, but until more analysis of organizational aspects of numerology is done, it's the best one going.

Fortunately, most of the work you do will be with individuals. Here there is a large corpus of experience to fall back on. In using the Ulian systemata and name variants, there are some lines of relationship which you should look for first. These lines will give you the clues you need to start your description, and once you have started, the rest is a lot easier. There are six places from which you can start.

Basic Numbers

This is the most common place to start, with the numbers of the name variants reduced to one digit. This gives a very general view of things to start with and gives you something to work from. It's where I started in the example above.

Start by seeing if there are any Impediments or Trial versus any Extending or Confirmations in the numbers. The more disharmony, the more difficult the person's life is likely to be. If two numbers are harmonious and the third not, then that third aspect of life is likely to be kept separate from the others. If all are harmonious, so much to the good.

It is also possible to get a case where all three are harmonious to one other number, but not both. For example, 7 is Confirming to 4, and 4 is Extending to 6, but 6 is Impediment to 7. This usually indicates a rather frustrating life, one often filled with quirks of psychology and inconsistent behaviour to anyone unaware of the different forces within the person.

Column Relations

It is also possible to start by examining all the numbers in the ones column, then the tens column, and then the hundreds column. In this you would be looking for variation between one name and another. For example, is someone outgoing in business (3 in the tens column of the Formal Name) and quiet in personal life (7 in the tens column of the Personal Name)? If so, you can guess much of his or her life will be wrapped around trying to preserve a wall between those two parts of a person's life.

Resonance Number

A resonant number is one with a pattern in its own numbers — which of course means it must be an extended number. If you find one, like 123 or 454 or 1221, then you can fruitfully begin your analysis with that particular number. In this way you would have a significant pattern which will lock impulses in one part of life with another. In this case we would expect the same influences appearing again and again in different aspects of the person's life. When this does occur, pay special attention to how the resonant number and the basic number derived from it relates to the Destiny Number.

Resonance Pattern

Closely related to the resonance number is the resonance pattern. It is much the same thing but the pattern is between the number and the number of each of the columns. For example, when you've got 3 in the tens (or second) column and 2 in the hundreds (or third) column, and so on. So, to carry through, 1234 is not only a resonance number but a resonance pattern as well. However, 3214 would still be a resonance pattern but would not be a resonance number, because each number leads to a different column, but there isn't a pattern to make it a resonance number.

(To be sure, take 3214 again: 4 is in the ones column, so go to column 4. In the fourth column is 3, so go to column 3. In the third column is 2, so go to column 2. In the second column is 1, so go to column 1 and start again.)

Repetition

Every time a number appears, whether in a basic or Extended position, it's significant. If a number keeps popping up — I usually take four or more times as significant — then it is likely to play a significant role in that person's life. In this case it doesn't matter in what position the number appears, just that it keeps reappearing.

Chains

If you find in one column of name variants all Extending numbers, and then find one of those numbers is Extending to the number next to it in the extended number, and this relationship keeps repeating, then the numbers can be taken as writing the sequence of narrative for you. And the same holds true if the relationship is Trial, Confirming, or Impediment.

So, for example, if you had the numbers in the ones column all Extending, and the number in the ones column of the Full Name is Extending to the number in the tens column of the Full Name, and then all the numbers in the tens column were Extending, you would have a very significant chain.

Just remember that the significance of the chain lasts as long as the chain lasts, but that the other numbers not in chain are to be included in your analysis as well.

Those are the six basic guidelines of what to look for. They are not meant to be rigid control, but guidelines of where to look, where you can hook into the chart.

However, there is another factor to be considered. This is the factor of vowels versus consonants which gives rise to the Head, Heart, and Hand numbers we've talked about before. These things we explore in the next chapter.

CHAPTER SEVEN

NAME ANALYSIS: PART TWO

One tool of numerology we owe almost entirely to the Jews and possibly as far back as Moses, is the separation of vowels and consonants and ascribing to each a different aspect of the self. This has been explained on the basis that in Hebrew they wrote only the consonants while the vowels had to be memorized, and therefore it was only natural that inner desires would be ascribed to the unwritten vowels and outer expression to the written consonants. I believe it closer to the truth to say the Jewish numerologists, or Cabbalists, had a coherent psychological theory long before Freud. And as pious men they discerned the relationship between this theory and the words and letters which they believed God had given to men as an expression of his will.

Whatever the origin of the tool, it still works and it still gives valuable service to numerologists. In the end, that is what counts. So we retain the division and the three types of number this gives rise to.

Heart Number
The Heart number is the value of the vowels of a name variant on their own. It represents the inner urges of a person; how they would like to be, how they would behave if there were no restrictions on them, their self image, how they imagine themselves doing things when they fantasize or visualize. This is how they wish to be.

Always remember that if there is no other vowel, then Y is used as the lone vowel.

Hand Number
This is the value of the consonants of a name variant. This is how

a person actually works when dealing with the world around them, the mask a person uses. This is the way or method a person goes about trying to get what he or she wants. It is the sort of permissions a person gives themself in which they can act, and so helps define the boundary between the possible and the impossible.

Head Number

This is all the letters of a person's name, both vowels and consonants. It is the totality of the person we are looking at. It is the Head number that describes how the person reconciles inner drive, hopes, fears, possibilities, and circumstances. It is always wise to examine the relationship of the Head number to the Hand and Heart number to see if a person is likely to be successful or not in reaching goals.

So, let's return to our hypothetical example in the last chapter, John Henry Hopkins. Whereas before we extended the numbers and did not limit ourselves to the basic numbers, here we go even further and have to look at the Head, Heart, and Hand numbers of each of the three name variants of the numeroscope. Thus:

Full Name

J   o   h   n   H   e   n   r   y   H   o   p   k   i   n   s

$10 + 60 + 8 + 50 + 8 + 5 + 50 + 90 + 700 + 8 + 60 + 70 + 20 + 9 + 50 + 100$

= 1298/2 Head Number

$10 \quad + 8 + 50 + 8 \quad + 50 + 90 + 700 + 8 \quad + 70 + 20 \quad + 50 + 100$

= 1164/3 Hand Number

$60 \quad\quad + 5 \quad\quad + 60 \quad + 9$

= 134/8 Heart Number

Formal Name

J   o   h   n   H   o   p   k   i   n   s

$10 + 60 + 8 + 50 + 8 + 60 + 70 + 20 + 9 + 50 + 100$

= 445/4 Head Number

$10 \quad + 8 + 50 + 8 \quad + 70 + 20 \quad + 50 + 100$

= 316/1 Hand Number

$60 \quad\quad + 60 \quad + 9$

= 129/3 Heart Number

Personal Name

J o h n

10 + 60 + 8 + 50 = 128/2 Head Number

10   + 8 + 50 = 68/5 Hand Number

   60   = 60/6 Heart Number

As you can see, there is a wealth of material in this systemata and, as mentioned in the last chapter, a number of things one can look for. A quick view of the numeroscope could provide the following analysis.

In the Full Name basic numbers we see Mr Hopkins' long term goals, fears, and hopes. They show he seeks some organizational achievement, a certain sense of power. From his hand number (3) we can see he tends to express these as a creative and expressive function in life. He shows a tendency to try to achieve his long term hopes by a certain glibness and, rather than plan, tends to look for luck to help him out. His real hopes, though, are shown by his 8 heart number, and here we see the hope for power, wealth, and sexual fulfilment (which would reinforce the 3 tendency to flirtation). Because 8 and 3 are trial numbers, we might have reason to doubt his success.

Look at the head number, a 2. This is what reconciles hopes with actions. Since 2 is Confirming to 8 but Impediment to 3 we can see further evidence of a slightly dissipative element to Mr Hopkins. Twos can be blasé, dependent, and tend to indulge in wishful thinking. This would reinforce the 3 tendency to be flighty and chaotic. But there is an element of wisdom and tact to him, and Mr Hopkins would be likely to show an industrious nature, working hard to achieve his long term goals. Where he might fail is through an inability to set concrete goals. Again, there seems to be an element of procrastination here, and this might prevent him from achieving the organizational, sexual, or even sensual goals he has set for himself.

The picture becomes clearer if we look at the Extended numbers of the Full Name. Notice how in the ones column (representing how he sees himself) we have strong reinforcements of his self-image as an organizational man; someone who wants to build something that will last. Indeed, both Heart and Hand number is 4, which emphasizes hard work and industry but at some expense of the creativity shown from the 3 Hand number. These 4s indicate that he is pragmatic about his long term goals and his ability to achieve them, but also that he is more likely to want to be kingmaker rather than king. He probably even has some image of the person he would like to be the frontman for. His Head number in the ones column is 8, which is also his basic Heart number. Again, we have a picture of the determined man, but we also see someone who would make others conform to his law rather than convince them of its value.

Remember that 8 is Trial to 4, so it is likely that some of the less reputable elements of 8 will be prominent. In this, look for a demand that others conform and an inability to forgive others for their weaknesses. A scenario of someone who sees themself or their way as perfect and any failure the fault of slackers.

If we look at the tens column, though, we see that when he deals with other people he is better equipped than his self-image might suggest. The Heart number in this column is 3, which leads us back to the basic Hand number, which shows he is willing to tell people about his ideas. He wants to deal with other people through enthusiasm, creativity, and even a bit of sparkle. Since all numbers in this column are Confirming numbers, when he's talking about his long term goals he is likely to put himself across very well. Many people, of course, seem rather listless or unimaginative until their favourite subject comes up. Suddenly, they are alive, quick, articulate. We haven't enough to say this is the case here, just that we would need to have a quick look at the tens column before deciding this man is eloquent.

Returning to this part of the chart, we would say that when Mr Hopkins does talk about his long term goals, his pitch is couched in terms of harmony, togetherness, and a streak of heart-and-home. There is still a workhorse element added in here, so when he deals with other people about his long term goals he has practical elements already worked out. In this, note the 6 parallels the 4s and the 8 in the ones column, and in fact is Extending to both. This piece of the puzzle shows us he believes his long term goals are definitely possible but only with the help and support of other people.

If we look back at the hundreds column and the Head number there, we see 9. This shows that when he deals with other people about his long term plans, when he is interacting with them as individuals, he deals with them from a position of humanity, liberality, concern, and wisdom. This is a far cry from the calculating and demanding self-image in the ones column Head number, reinforced by the basic Heart number. From this we can suggest the plans of liberality and community for Mr Hopkins extends only to those people who like his ideas. Other than that he may tend to go a bit sour on people, possibly leading to the opinion, 'either you are his friend, or you are not'.

However, if you look at the hundreds column you will see that the Heart and Hand numbers are both 1, but the Head number is 2, and Impediment. In other words, when revealing himself to the world he tries to look enthusiastic and dynamic when he should be trying to be wise and tactful. He is more concerned with himself and the impression he is trying to make than what he is actually trying to say. So, though he gets his message across (as seen from the tens column) it's not the message he needs to get across if he is going to get the support he needs to achieve his long term goals. In other words, he is able to present himself, and to actually act, as the person he believes he has to be to get where he ultimately wants to go, but his perception of what he should be like is all wrong. He should concentrate more on being a referee of others, not a ramrod, if he is to get anywhere in the world.

If we return to the basic Hand number, 3, we see it reinforces the hundreds column Hand and Heart numbers because they are an Extension of 3. However, 2 is Impediment to 3. This would serve to reinforce the opinion of John Hopkins as trying to look like a go-getter, a gregarious person who's fun to be around but who has a bit of trouble getting out of the limelight. If he centred his attention on others a bit more, he would be better off. Quite possibly his enthusiasm comes in spurts of great creativity followed by the blasé inactivity of the 2.

But 2 itself reinforces the self-image of the ones column and the basic Head and Heart numbers. Now less the organizational 4 or 8, 2 is still Extension to both. It emphasizes the need to do things in their own time, in their proper place in the cycle. This reinforces the ideas of spurts of activity mooted in the above paragraph. The Earth-mother 2 does have a cycle of seasons, but not as much as lunar 6. However, 2 is also very much a family number, and again we return to a concept of 'we'. I would say from this that John Hopkins has a goal in mind that includes more than himself. He is thinking of the family or a similar 'we' group and hopes to see that group succeed through his own dynamic activities if only other people will support him in the way he wants them to.

So the tens column is reinforced by the basic Hand number, 3, while the ones and hundreds column is not so unified. This means that there is some chance that John Henry Hopkins will reach his long term goals, but there may be difficulties in his way. But, we will investigate this a bit more, later.

(By the way, we have now spent about twice as much time on just one name variant with Head, Heart, and Hand numbers than we spent in the last chapter on all three name variants. It's very possible to write individual numeroscopes longer than this book.)

Now, let's take a look at the Formal Name and begin with a quick view of the basic numbers. These show a person who wants to be creative and innovating, who in business, social, and political life wants to fulfil some real needs of other people. When he talks about this hope, he displays real enthusiasm for his job. We see this from his 3 Heart and 1 Hand number, numbers which extend each other. However, his Head number is 4, Confirming to 1 but Impediment to 3, an ambiguous situation.

I would say Mr Hopkins succeeds in this area of his life but not in the context or the way he wants. In other words he is a good campaign manager who wants to be the candidate, or a good manager who remembers happier days as a salesman. Much of this, though, depends not only on the Destiny Number, but which company, party or whatever he works with.

As can be seen from the basic Hand number, he does express himself as enthusiastic and dynamic, as has been mentioned, but his 4 Head number shows concern that the organization succeeds in its own goals. In other words, he has hopes and fears that he keeps in tight reign so he can pursue the goals of the organization, whether it be a business, party, or social milieu.

So this is one part of life where John Hopkins has subsumed personal goals and accentuated the goals of others, which may be the source of the frustration noted in this part of his life as mentioned in the last chapter. This is something that reinforces the possibility he will never get to his long term goals, and that those long term goals do not involve this part of his life. We will get a better idea, though, if we look at the same numbers in their Extended forms.

In the ones column we see how his self-image is set; how he sees himself in the business and social world. He wants to be a person who shows a grasp of broad principles, who is curious and willing to learn and, by the way, is an experimental lover. This we see from the 9 in the Heart number of the ones column.

Yet, from the 6 Hand number, we see that when he imagines himself trying to carry out these hopes, they are expressed in hopes of gregarious joy, drawing together. In this we see an echo of his long term goals when focused on dealing with other people (Full Name's tens column Hand number). Where the difference sets in is the Head number.

The ones column Head number of the Formal Name is five. Mr Hopkins sees himself achieving different things and entering different fields. He may try to star in too many shows to achieve great success in any one of them. It would take quick wit, ability to think quickly, and perhaps a bit of chicanery to keep his self-image intact when he actually deals with reality. In short, he may try to be a bit too much. I say this because 5 is Impediment to 6 and Trial to 9 and it is mediator to those two.

When dealing with other people in this area of life, John Hopkins wants to get along, to be known as a person of patience, loyalty, and a good deputy, hence the 2 in the tens column Heart number. When he actually gets down to dealing with other people, though, he is rather excitable, friendly, enthusiastic, but a bit self-centred. A typical 1, in other words. It's as if he believes that if he is excited about something, you will be excited about it, too, or will at least pretend to be in order not to be left out.

In trying to blend these two notions together, he comes up with a 4 Head number. Again, to overcome these Impediments he puts his organizational face on; the stern, efficient man. Four is Extending to 2 and Confirming to 1, but 1 is Impediment to 2, so he is actually set well in this field so long as his conversation is organized for him. In this case he is probably talking about business-related matters, so this pre-organized element is normally provided for him.

To reinforce this idea, let's look at the hundreds column where the Heart number (1) is Extending to the Hand number (3) and the Head number (4) is Extending to the Heart but Impediment to the Hand number. In other words, we are looking at the image he is likely to project whatever it is he actually tries to do.

It is likely that the image he hopes for will elude him, but the image he really has won't hurt him. He may want to look like a dynamic go-getter, a pioneer who clinches the deal, but he will look like the happy-go-lucky sort whose luck overcomes a tendency to lack planning and, occasionally, skill. Because of that, he will still be considered valuable to the organization.

Again, we could go on from here, but by now it should be obvious that in numeroscopes you can deliniate very precise areas of interest of a person, and how they are likely to succeed in those areas. It should also be obvious that most numeroscopes will have a 'thread' or theme that will be repeated again and again as you look first to one area and then another.

In the above example we kept tripping over enthusiasm (1, 3, 9) coupled with hopes of wisdom and togetherness (2, 6) being used within a frame of reference of organizational concerns (4, 8). Notice how 7 never shows up, 5 appears once, while 1 is in there eight times in all.

However, to get the best look at someone, you need their Destiny Number, and that's what we study next.

CHAPTER EIGHT

THE NAME AND THE DESTINY NUMBERS

In most numeroscopes, the relationship between the Name and Destiny numbers will be the crux of your analysis. It is unfortunate that this is also the hardest part to be able to do correctly. So, in this chapter, we will begin with looking at part of the numeroscope of John Henry Hopkins, only this time we will give him a birthdate of, say, 13 January 1956. In the second part of the chapter, we will outline the most important points to remember in each of the 81 possible combinations of a Name and a Destiny Number.

Numeroscope

John Henry Hopkins

Destiny Data

Birthdate 13 01 1956	Destiny Number	1970 / 8
Day Aspect		13 / 4
Month Aspect		1
Year Aspect		1956 / 3

Name Data

Name Numbers	Head	Hand	Heart
Full Name	1298 / 2	134 / 8	1164 / 3
Formal Name	445 / 4	129 / 3	316 / 1
Personal Name	128 / 2	60 / 6	68 / 5

Distribution of Numbers   *Case Typology*

				Fu.N.	F.N.	P.N.
1 × 2	4 × 0	7 × 2	Head numbers	+	−	+
2 × 2	5 × 4	8 × 3	Hand numbers	+	−	+
3 × 0	6 × 2	9 × 2	Heart numbers	−	+	−

We will begin with the bottom part of this chart, since it provides convenient guy-lines to the overview of the numeroscope. In the typology, we will look only at the Head numbers. As in Chapter 2, we discover a person likely to be successful in minor things or in helping others, but unlikely to be able to bring things together for themselves. In particular, there are frustrations in the business sector of life. If we couple this with the distribution of numbers, we discover John will have trouble with creativity (lack of threes) and in organizing himself (lack of fours).

These problems fly directly in the face of his year aspect. As a 3 itself, it indicates the very lessons he must learn are those bound with creativity, enthusiasm, and an ability to let his hair down. Already, there is indication he has shown trouble in meeting his spiritual lesson in life.

Let's turn to his Full Name. The Head number is harmonious with his Destiny Number (hereafter called D.N.), with 2 being Extending to 8. The Full Name number, or Head number, in turn, is Extending to the Hand number but Impediment to his Heart number. The Heart and Hand numbers, by the way are Trial. This is actually a good configuration, but not in the short term.

Again, we are shown a man rather divided between inspiration and organization, emotion and logic. Because 8 and 2 are Extending, it will show John Hopkins as a man who prefers logic and proof. He will not like to trust his hunches.

In this, I would guess he took a desk job with its daily rations of boredom and steady money rather than risk that security with some creative or self-fulfilling job. In this, he is like many people, but I would think that the strong division in his chart indicates the conflict will come to a head.

In the meantime, John won't use his instincts unless he is pushed.

He prefers to do things as they have always been done, and ought to remember that to 'organize' is to 'make like a living thing'.

It would seem, too, that John will finally achieve his long term goals, but not the vital spiritual demands made upon him. Look, for example, at the ones column of his Extended Fu.N. numbers. These show the self-image of a man who wants to be organized but (because of the lack of 4s in the distribution) feels he isn't sufficiently precise in his life. He acts in what he hopes is an organized manner (Hand number) and sees organization as the means to doing things (8 Head number). All reinforcing, but the year aspect is 6 and the D.N. is 0; where do these fit in?

In terms of his spiritual lesson, his self-image is extending to his actions and hopes and the reconciliation between the two. This indicates he will have an evolving self-image, one which will, during his life, grow more and more realistic and more and more inclined to the needs of the spiritual lesson. In terms of his overall lesson, his self-image means very little. In other words, his 6 in the year aspect shows he will internalize his spiritual lesson, and will come to accept the need for the freedom and creativity of 3. However, combined with what we have seen before, we would have to suggest he will learn this lesson very late in life. Before then, destiny demands that that need be held in abeyance so he can fulfil the organizational desires he has.

During this earlier period, he is likely to feel more comfortable with the results of inspiration than the process itself. Artists and mystics will, during this time, put him ill-at-ease since he will see in them the embodiment of inspiration. He is likely to dismiss both as being useless, impractical, or even parasitical on people who do 'real' work. From this we can suggest a fair karmic backlog which has to be cleared before he can begin going forward again.

This unease with inspiration refers back to the lack of threes in his name. But there is another element to this. There is a slightly dissipative element to him, since 8 and 3 are both sexual numbers. He probably sees sex as part of a power relationship, and operates on the assumption that the more sex, the more power. Thinking of the legends of Zeus' gambolling, this does not seem entirely out of the blue.

These tensions will appear in his self-image, in his thoughts about himself when he thinks in the long term. He will begin life seeking to organize his actions. He will believe that he must become more efficient, handle things by a schedule, and establish the logic of his hopes and the honesty of others — to be 'on square' with them and be sure they are the same with him. He will do his best to achieve exactly this, but when attempting to do so, he will see these things fall apart. (That is, 4 Heart and Hand numbers Trial to 8 Head number.)

They are, however, all numbers extending to the ones column of the year aspect. On this we would suggest that he sees this as the way to achieve his long term goals and encompass his spiritual lesson. However, the divisions in his chart show that those long term goals are divorced from the actual procedures he is going through in his early life. What he is trying to do with his life, even if successful, will not take him where he wants to go. This is reinforced looking at the basic numbers of the Fu.N.

As we have seen, the 3 Heart number shows he wants to be a creative, enthusiastic, happy-go-lucky person. With others he would like to be gregarious and attentive. When trying to achieve these sorts of things, though, his 8 Hand number shows he tries to use unsuitable methods. He becomes square jawed, determined, and hard-working. Perhaps he has a belief that fun is somehow sinful, and though he would like to get in the swim of things, he does not seem to believe he should do it. He turns his thoughts to the responsibilities he takes on his shoulders and those he puts on everyone else's.

His Head number, 2, is Confirming to 8 but Impediment to 3. This shows that the results of that struggle comes much more on the hands of organization and responsibility than fun. He has built strong defences against his hopes, and purely from experience I would suggest his hope parallels some experience in childhood where his hopes were dashed due to someone else's better organization or strength or power. In addition, one or both parents probably put it in his head that he has to 'be responsible' and to 'shoulder the burden'.

The ones column numbers shows how very far he has internalized these images, but even a cursory look at the tens column, looking at how he deals with other people, shows that the old image is still there. We are getting more and more the image of John as a person trying to get out of his shell.

Note the 6 Heart number in the tens column, showing that in dealing with people, John is concerned with harmony and, still, responsibility. There is an aspect of togetherness in the way John wants to deal with people in relation to his long term goals in life. His actions in this field, the 3 Hand number, shows the very enthusiasm and excitement he is supposed to learn but finds inhibitions stopping him. The Head number, a 9, shows that the reconciliation (as if one were needed) between these two is the humanitarian and teaching aspects of existence. This is the only case of three Confirming numbers in John Hopkins' chart.

Although I advised you before that Destiny Numbers are related only to Head numbers, I'm going to show here I lied by looking at the tens column of the year aspect and the tens column of the D.N. and relate them back.

I have spoken of a change in this man's life, and I've said before that he seems to believe people are essential to his achievement of his long term goals. The tens column of the year aspect indicates that dealing with other people is the abrasive that breaks down his organized, logical self-image and lets loose the earlier, more natural self-image. The 5 in this column is entirely at odds with what John is trying to project, achieve, and be. The 5 shows dealing with others in a mercurial, interested, and entirely spontaneous nature. The same goes for his D.N., a 7, which is pulling him away from other people and towards introspection, providing a vantage point of observation of self.

His relations with others, then, would tend to be successful, and people would tend to like him when they meet or deal with him in this sort of situation. That the year aspect and D.N. pull from that should not bother us greatly. It is more that success in this area will show how he has been going at things wrong.

There will come a point in John's life when someone will bring up the discrepancies in him. And, having done so, will bring about a major change in his life. The organizational needs, perhaps by now achieved, will fall away and he will go through a dramatic change in life. It will probably include a change of life-style, career, and perhaps even where he lives.

This is reinforced by the basic numbers of the Formal Name. The

Head number is disharmonious with the D.N., yet Confirming to the month aspect and, incidentally, the Heart number. This would indicate success in the outer forms of the business/social/political hierarchies. Turning this back to the Full Name discussions, we get the picture of the man who has succeeded in his youthful goals, who suddenly finds it wasn't really what he wanted all along. It is often a trick of destiny to let a person know they don't want something by letting them have it to the fullest. This almost certainly seems to be the case here.

Going back to the Full Name, we can look at the image John Hopkins presents when dealing with his long term goals. The Heart number of the hundreds column is 1, so he wants to present the image of a person who is dynamic, pioneering, energetic, and so on. His hundreds column Hand number shows he goes about presenting that image in the right way. Yet his hundreds column Head number is 2, which means people actually see him as wise, tactful, and inclined to be dependent on other people, hard-working, but occasionally blasé about things. Such a discrepancy should give us pause. We could explain it in terms of his dealing with other people — the 9 tens column Head number providing wisdom and tact, for example. However, there is also something in the D.N. and year aspect we should take note of.

Both, as usually happens, have the same number in the hundreds column, 9. The lesson of presentation is the same for most people in any one era of an age, and the same is the case here. John is impelled to discover about humanity, liberality, and kindness. His spiritual lesson is bound in the concepts of initiation and allowing others their path to the secrets of the universe. In responding to that universal imperative, he accepts the value of others by accepting initiation as a process of a group rather than individuals. He sees it as the need to keep the link to the source open. Others react to this in him, and see through the image he tries to project.

By doing this, he has set up the dialectic of his life. He accepts others and their value, but seems unable to understand how these independent individuals will achieve what he wants to achieve. Believing this to be a problem, accepting his dependence on what seems undependable, he tries to compensate by his organizational concerns. He is trying to bind people to his dream because he believes they won't do so voluntarily.

The only way to learn, really, is to make up about 20 names and birth dates and do the numeroscopes for each. Begin with no more than the basic numbers, then go on to the extended numbers, then the Head, Heart, and Hand numbers for each name variant, then the Destiny Number, and finally the Destiny Number and its aspects related to each of the numbers. Only when you have done all these, pick on real people you know and see if what you come up with is actually right. Even then, drop back to a simpler level and build up again.

I have advised you not to relate Head, Heart, and Hand number systems back to the Destiny Number and then went ahead and did so. Simply, though it looks easy if you've done it for a long time, it is an area where beginners will make the most appalling mistakes. Using the aspects of the D.N. with the Heart and Hand numbers is getting into very specific details of how a person thinks and acts. Making a mistake here can skew your entire chart, and that can have disastrous consequences. Just wait until you've had practice before getting into that end of the pool.

Destiny and Name Numbers

Destiny Number 1 and Name Number

1 (Confirming). Like any coincidence of these two numbers, the faults and virtues are reinforced and likely to make for a seemingly eccentric personality. A life of ups and downs. Think of a pioneer woodsman, with no society to reign in his excesses or to fall back upon. These people are the epitomé of the hard-working, outgoing, egotistic personality. For this person, the lessons of temperance and patience are especially important and especially hard to learn. Intuition must be accepted on its own terms, and no attempt must be made to make it a slave of this person's whims.

2 (Impediment). Impelled to energy, enthusiasm, and extroversion, is met with quietude, reserve, and independence. This person needs to question less and do more, to get involved and be a self-starter. There is also a tendency to meditate facts in a new form, but facts have to be faced as they are. Every person has limits, and these people must accept theirs. Rather than deny limits, accept them and then grow to

fit what is needed. In these people, diplomacy is dulled, being largely a well-timed kick in the pants, but at least bootlicking is also excluded. Should stick up for self quite well. Will be a hard life for these people.

3 (Extending). Unhesitating, irresistible sometimes, these people have a dash of charisma, boundless energy, creativity, intuition and inspiration, and a tendency to believe 'I love me and the hell with everybody else'. With an almost Bacchanal worldview, these people are often in danger of dissipating their talents. Quick to anger and slow to forgive, they should learn to see themselves as a condensation of their environments. They build up things easily, but then watch them fall apart because they didn't cement the structure together. These people have an eventful life, but one without anything lasting behind it.

4 (Confirming). A well balanced personality, with enthusiasm and sobriety in mixed proportions, ambition to succeed but a deep-seated patience. Persevering and self-starting, these people are rarely pioneers. The ideas they have they prefer to hone and test out before putting into practice. Similarly, intuition and logic must agree. Intuitive thoughts are something to work backwards from and, if the chain isn't complete, is often disregarded. Many people with this configuration have a wry humour which can lead to cynicism. They tend to have a good life, but not one extremely notable for world-changing success.

5 (Trial). These people tend to be a collection of disjointed weaknesses and strengths. Enthusiastic and pioneering, everything else about these people tend to operate of their own accord. Lacking patience to bring anything about, their many ideas are things just tossed off in conversation. They jump from trend to trend, idea to idea. Avoids the egoism of 1, and is able to understand their limits, but inclined to forget those limits in the heat of the moment and take on too much. A difficult life which can be turned around at about middle age.

6 (Trial). These people are likely to lead a rough life, but others will see the effort they make. They often nag as a means of keeping others at bay and have trouble accepting responsibility for their own actions. Yet they understand the message in being a condensation of their environments, and development in later life is common. Begins life

petty and often both vengeful and spiteful, but eventually discovers people react to this and this is why these people are often lonely. These people often face a crisis in life in their twenties over this. Easily influenced by others, so if they get in with the best of people they can put out 110 per cent of themselves.

7 (Confirming). Normally energetic in youth, by middle age a wry humour comes out. The focus turns from action to achievement and a loss of egotism. A good and effective life that combines the pragmatic with the ideal. These people have learned humility, but patience is still a hard lesson.

8 (Extending). A strong combination, these people are highly emotional but keep those emotions on a tight reign. They are hard-working, pioneering, and willing to accept their place in the universe. Though they don't take things personally and are slow to anger, they can make dangerous enemies. They can be moody, at once friendly and outgoing and then suddenly aloof. They are stubborn, even single-minded to a fault and unable to know when to quit, but they often bring home the bacon when nobody else thought it was even worth trying. They will make their own course in life, and can achieve quite a bit, but will face powerful opposition.

9 (Impediment). These people see in the universal principles a good method of personal gain, which in itself is fine. However, they are caught in the concept of the ego or 'glorious I' and the fallacy that, if the self reflects eternal laws, then the self is necessarily eternal. Naturally, these people create problems for themselves. They are friendly and willing to share with others. In later life, they can gain a maturity that doesn't lack the enthusiasm of youth. For all their faults, they have a degree of luck that keeps them from hitting bottom. Nevertheless, these people are not likely to have a good life.

Destiny Number 2 and Name Number

1 (Impediment). These people tend to be bullies. They are self-starters, but they are undisciplined and dissipate their energies in pleasing others or harrassing them. These people are in danger of losing contact with

the source of things in the mistaken belief that, if it's broken, it won't be hard to get it back again. Naturally disinclined to having a good life, the link with the source can keep them going in something like the right direction. These people are friendly and make good listeners, but they are completely unable to handle the problems of others. They tend to heavily indulge in fantasy, and this is a source of creativity for them.

2 (Confirming). Tactful and extremely loyal, these are people who are likely to do fairly well in their life. Again, the best and the worst is possible, but the worst is usually mitigated. Tends to tell white lies to make things 'more interesting'. Receptive to new ideas, but judges and applies them by their merits. Tends to have a good life, but largely one lived for, or through, others.

3 (Impediment). These people are concerned about others, and they tend to have a wide circle of friends and acquaintances, but they never seem to have any old friends. Their friendships and loves never seem to last that long, perhaps because these people fluctuate so much between jollity and reserved dignity. These people are subjective about their own abilities or the worth of their own ideas. They are nervous people who fear putting a foot wrong, even when there are no grounds for this fear. These two things make them hyper-critical about the ideas of others, and brash about the worth of their own ideas. They have 20-20 hindsight, and 'always knew' what they should have done. These people are set for a shaky life, one full of disappointment.

4 (Extending). A watchful and cautious person who plays life like a game of chess. Often manipulative, sometimes a kingmaker who controls things from behind the scenes, these people nevertheless remain loyal to those around them. They love the home and the family and tend to centre their lives around them. Tends to have a materialist philosophy and prefer logical proof to anything that even smacks of inspiration. It is not enough that the thing works, it must be seen how it works. These people have a consistent personality from youth to late middle age, but thereafter they tend to become more introspective and fantasize more. In all, they live an eventful life.

5 (Confirming). These people have an enthusiasm harness and are directed by pragmatism. They will give a new idea every chance, but if the idea doesn't work under optimum conditions, then out it goes. More, they only want to hear about ideas that will affect them, directly. They know their limits, and know when to move from one thing to another. They aren't inclined to be flighty or to fight for hopeless causes. They spend the majority of their lives seeking a link to the source, and, when they have got it, use it as a base for exploring the world. The image of a travelling Knight of the Grail appertains, here. These are people who are likely to have the good life, but one tinged with a certain sadness.

6 (Trial). Steady, patient, and reliable, they seem set to have a good life, but they become workhorses for everybody else, for they are also pernickety, stubborn, nagging, and all too willing to become the victims to other peoples' plans. In early life, things seem to go well, but in later life things tend to get bogged down. They just keep going on with whatever worked in their youth with no regard for changes in events, the times, or in themselves. There is an element of immaturity here. They can also turn to fantasy and like that more than the reality. They tend to have rough lives, but caused by themselves.

7 (Trial). These people find the world confusing, and so withdraw from it rather than try to understand it. They tend to accept whatever was the last opinion put to them, simply because they don't really have opinions of their own. This makes them appear to be boot-lickers to others. Undiplomatic, unwilling to listen to others, these people apply the universal laws only outside themselves, and want the world to change much so they won't have to change even a little. If that happens, their unpleasant life can wind up being rather more satisfying than would be expected.

8 (Confirming). These people have two basic rules; 'Put yer back into it' and 'Give a sucker an even break'. They combine the ability for strong leadership with a desire to see others grow, yet they are more likely to be in a supporting rather than a commanding position. Though patient and diplomatic, better not to push them too far, for they have

a strong sense of justice that can make them fierce fighters. No matter how much they do, these people are still unsatisfied. Beginning work early, they build up to an intense pitch, and continue working until relatively late in life.

9 (Extending). These people live interesting lives, full of events and effort. They have strong links to the source and nurture these links over time. Sometimes, they think they can see beyond the links and into the source itself. They are intuitive, creative, and sometimes adventurous. They like to travel. They believe in balance and temperance as ideals, but these are more often observed in breach than practice. Their early lives are full of frustration for them, but from late youth on they tend to get a grip on things and soar without seeming effort.

Destiny Number 3 and Name Number
1 (Extending). Extroverted, fresh, lively, entertaining, but tending to be self-centred if not actually egotistic. In some ways these people are divine fools who may not believe they are the centre of the universe but do admit to believing they are the centre of their own universe, their own experiences. They are self-starters and inclined to enjoy the new over the old. They have the determination to see things through. They make good talkers and good listeners. Quick to anger, they are also fast to forgive, but once an enemy they are never a friend. These people have a good life, especially in their youth.

2 (Impediment). They are happy-go-lucky to a fault, and seemingly impervious to the moods of others. They are too immersed in the moment to use any wisdom they have, and instead maintain a sensuous personality that enjoys all the physical pleasures. Though creative, they know that creativity is dependent on something, or someone else, and therefore never put their ideas into practice, but just toss them off in conversation. In many ways, their happy-go-lucky stance covers the moodiness this dependence generates. In all, they have an unhappy and ineffectual life.

3 (Confirming). Their lives will be happy, but will achieve very little

of note. They are tricksters and pranksters one minute, and a full-blown Jupiter Optimus Maximus the next. If they are not with the one they love, they love the one they are with. They are creative and energetic, but tend to stop when they have mastered the skill rather than when they have completed the task at hand. Yet there is a certain dignity about them, even when they are their most jovial. Indeed, many times the fun-loving youth turns into the dignified, almost statesman-like character of middle age, and then into the contemplator of old age.

4 (Impediment). Reserved quite often, but when they become happy and boisterous, they tend to overdo it. These are people who always seem to be slightly out of tune with others. In the same way, they have trouble understanding their own intuitions. They will argue them down with logic and be wrong, or follow the hunch against logic and be wrong. This same hesitancy prevents them from carrying out many of their plans. They will have an unhappy life, one full of contradictions and about faces. This is especially so in their twenties and through to their forties.

5 (Extending). Happy and lucky, they give no thought for tomorrow because they believe tomorrow can fend for itself. They see change as good because they see things as not good enough now, but they never go in for change for its own sake. They tend to like mythology, fantasy, and folklore. In their early lives, they tend to be activity oriented, travelling from one place to another, getting experience in one thing or another. By middle age they begin to put this together into a coherent view of the world which then lasts them into a usually advanced old age.

6 (Confirming). These people are very home orientated. They love fellowship, harmony, hospitality, and a good party. But they have also a very strong sense of responsibility, and very much want to raise a family. Their leadership abilities and enthusiasm leads them to a good life with some measure of achievement in it. These people tend to mate for life, and often live through their children.

7 (Trial). Self-contradictory people, really, they tend to withdraw from other people and then fret about the lack of company, then to draw

people together and want to get rid of them. Over-indulgent in fantasy, they can become more interested in fantasy than the reality. In all, they are likely to have a bad life, but with all the 'debts' owing to karma being put off until later and later in life until it catches up. These people take the universal laws as if they were fraternity rules. Take care, for they don't keep their word unless it's convenient.

8 (Trial). They want power, but can't handle it. Sexually active, they remain alone and unhappy. They tend to be organizational toadies; people who have no beliefs except organizational efficiency and the embodiment of the organization in its leadership. However reliable they are to superiors, they can be double-dealing and scheming with equals and those below them. If they are to make anything of their lives other than hollow ladder climbing, they will have to learn to understand justice as a metaphysical concept. They must see that when they harm others, they are harming themselves as well.

9 (Confirming). Under an easy going manner and quiet laughter lies an iron-willed visionary. These are people who meditate on life, who fit their enthusiasm and inspiration into an entire magical or philosophical worldview. They are concerned with the growth of themselves and others. Yet there is an element of reserve to them, for in many ways they are wanderers, questors for something. They seek to observe the world as well as participate in it, for they are laying in stores for their next lifetime.

Destiny Number 4 and Name Number
1 (Confirming). These are people who like to do everything for themselves, from pioneering the idea to completing the project. This means they often get too much on their plates, so though they are frequently successful, they are just as often harried and frustrated. They are objective about themselves, always wanting to achieve things but doing so in the right manner. They are in some ways traditionalists, keeping to the way things ought to be done. Though they like others to be comfortable, they are themselves rather spartan by nature. They will have a life of good work and some success.

2 (Extending). These are steady people, who believe in rectitude and

who can generally be relied upon to keep their word. They aren't given
to rash promises or quick opinions, and they will get their back up
if they are pushed and become moody and sullen. These people need
to be alone quite often. Hard workers, sometimes habit ridden though
never really in a rut, they make better lieutenants than leaders. They
are loyal, determined, and concerned about health and home. They
will lead quiet but important lives, where they quietly build up
something of significance that lasts after they have gone.

3 (Impediment). Consistent, compulsive hoarders, they don't give out
their ideas or goods or love. Because of this they lead frustrated and
enclosed lives of little note. This is less of a problem in early youth,
because they enjoy a good time and little else is expected of them at
that age. However, they take responsibility badly. They are impulsive,
as buyers and givers, and often regret it later. These are people with
a hurt who often seem to be looking for something to make it all 'OK'
again.

4 (Confirming). A bureaucrat world might suit these people, except
they are too interested in solving the problem to be so bogged down
in process. They like things ordered and neat and don't want to be
changed or hurried along. They are not self-starters, but once they
do begin, they finish the job. They are loyal to friends and superiors,
and are likely to get married late in life, and probably to someone of
a different age group.

5 (Impediment). Too flighty to ever complete their plans, these people
tend to dream of grand things but never bother to bring it all back
to what they can do about the matter right now. They are people who
observe the world, often in minute detail, but never really come to
grips with what it means. This all means they do not achieve very
much in their lives. Even their circle of friends is no more than a wide
circle of acquaintances, for these people cannot be trusted nor do they
trust anyone.

6 (Extending). Responsible and friendly, these people like to keep to
the quieter side of things. In many ways they are home-bodies, but
they also probably have every home entertainment module they can

afford. The home, after all, is an extension of the self. Orderly and neat, they are not compulsive cleaners, though may tend to become so as they move on into older age. The centring on the family means the success of children counts as much as their own success, so they pour a lot into being parents. On the whole, they will live a good and worthy life.

7 (Confirming). A withdrawn sort of people who are good listeners but rather ineloquent, themselves. They build up their lives slowly, developing their life's work over time. They see this work not as a thing in itself, but something to be handed down to later generations. They are thus more successful later in life, spending the early time learning and developing and the latter part actually building. Strong artistic leanings, but leanings which usually go unfulfilled. Tend to mystic visions, but subjects those visions to a logical regimen. Rather happy with their lives.

8 (Trial). These people are equipped with a lot of natural power, but they don't have the plans to match them. The excess energy 'burns off' and can cause a great deal of damage. Their goals are so important to them that they often lose sight of the importance of justice or self-determination. They will have to gain a greater sense of proportion and, incidentally, a bit more loyalty to people and less loyalty to doing things by the book. Too often blames failures on other people, can be 98 and still starting off, 'If it weren't for my childhood . . .' A life spent making plans and being frustrated and failing despite working hard. Learn to shoot for targets that can be hit.

9 (Trial). These people are a case of visionaries trying to escape their own vision. They can achieve much in their youth, but in middle age a certain sloth sets in. They try being chaotic in order to be free, they do not plan to be spontaneous, they do not give orders so others can enjoy the same. They must realize there are reasons for these things existing. They must become less wrapped up in themselves, less concerned that, if the initiates operate a certain way, then everybody should — without training. They are essentially dependent on others, and if this isn't recognized, their lives will be mis-spent and lacklustre.

Destiny Number 5 and Name Number

1 (Trial). Though optimistic and hard-working, they achieve very little. Partly this is because they are too eager to kick over the old in favour of the new and to take a chance on a new spin of the wheel of fate. They tend to pick apart philosophies and just grab what will support their cause of the moment. They always have to have a cause as a means of making themselves more important in their own eyes. They have a lot of friends, but never ones that last long. They need to always have something new going on, and old friends do not offer that. Not a rough life, but one that seems to drift along without real basis or real happiness.

2 (Confirming). These are people who will probably spend their youth jumping from one thing to another, will build up a career or lifestyle in middle age, and then continue to reap the benefits well into old age. They work hard and accept change fairly easily. Though truthful in most things, they tend to be a bit cavalier with the facts when the matter involved is unimportant. They are open to change, but only at the right time for them, the old must be completed and put away before the new is begun. They have a streak of the gambler in them, and they tend to have an intense internal life with rich and varied fantasies.

3 (Extending). Enthusiastic, inspired, and dynamic, these people have a real need to learn to be able to settle down. Their ideas are often good, and get included in the projects of others. Thus they often achieve quite a bit in their lives even if they don't appear to do so. If they complete their own projects, they will have an easier old age than would otherwise be the case. They are naturally people who don't follow trends but who impose trends of their own. And though they act the fool, they can still take others for all they've got. Yet, they don't suffer fools gladly, and are rather contemptuous of fools, altogether. And, a third contradiction, they are humanitarian and willing to help anyone in genuine need. But for all this they will lead happy, enjoyable lives.

4 (Impediment). These are people who leap before they look; they come up with an idea (or steal someone else's) and try to put it into

practice before doing any planning or study about it. When the chips are down, they will lie because they want something so badly and have failed so often. Their early lives are likely to be hard, and their later lives uneventful. Yet, they do make some real attempts at improvement. They are hard, if rather sporadic, workers, and their attempts at improvement can, with guidance, have some real effects.

5 (Confirming). Quick witted and wilful, these people are also sly and wily; the sort of people you love or hate but can never ignore. For all this, there is a naïvety to them, the trickster who sees the world but does not comprehend. Early life is full of fun and they establish themselves in the world, but from middle age on they become more and more introspective, more willing to try to piece together what they have been witnessing. 'I've just realized . . .' becomes a common expression. It is later in life that they begin to specialize, to accept their own limitations in this world. They are people who lead decent, if rather hectic, lives.

6 (Impediment). They cannot accept responsibility, and they distrust people, so there is very little harmony in their lives. They are absent minded and often they are slobs, leaving everything where they last used it. As children these people need a firm hand and discipline, as adults they need a careful regime to keep in check their occasionally workshy habits. If they volunteer to do something then one must make certain that they deliver. They do pay attention to detail, but often in a haphazard manner, citing detail in one place but not another. In all, people who live an unhappy, unfulfilled life.

7 (Extending). They have a nervous, restless energy that seems to take them everywhere, always experimenting, trying everything once. They spend their youth building up a worldview based on personal experience and sometimes their own inner visions. In their youth they are likely to try new religions, new causes, become politically active, or go overseas as part of an aid programme. In middle age they use that information and worldview to build up their own activities in the world. They are often apart from others, though seemingly in the midst of people. This, too, is part of their observing the world. They will lead a rather hard life, but one full of achievement and enjoyment for them.

8 (Confirming). These are people who like to keep a finger on the pulse of things; they observe, put many small facts together, and go from there. They make deadly enemies, but they are not inclined to keep grudges. Simply, they put a line between what's theirs and what isn't, and won't allow any trespass. Rather hard working, they are inclined to jump from one thing to another trying to do everything for themselves, and thus overwork themselves. In the first half of life this is not a significant problem, because it can all add to experience, but in later life it can cause various health problems to crop up. However, though they live a hard life, the standards imposed are their own, and they find it satisfying.

9 (Trial). The visions come so fast, they don't follow any to the end, but turn them into a sort of entertainment. The same with the great principles. Humanitarianism and charity are agreed to, but are quickly forgotten in the heat of the moment. These are people who follow the crowd rather than think things through for themselves. They enjoy travel, in mind or body, and this can lead to a broadening of horizons. Indeed, these people could benefit from some time alone to discover how they feel about things so they can turn their life from a hard one to one with real potential.

Destiny Number 6 and Name Number

1 (Trial). Generally, these people are too egotistical to practise harmony, but they are fully willing to take responsibility for what they do. They are hard working, and can become 'all work and no play' sorts shortly before having a heart attack. They do better in life if they have a spouse or coach, etc., who handles all the basic requirements of day-to-day living. They have an ability to follow through with a plan, going one step at a time, but circumstances seem to always prevent the consummation of their desires. They need to learn the cycles of things before they can start to live a happy life. Without this, they are likely to lead lives which are disappointing and touched by tragedy.

2 (Trial). They retreat into fantasy rather than take responsibility for their own actions. In particular, they tend to 'rewrite' their memories to make them better coincide with their own desires. They are willing

to shatter harmony to get their own way, and they don't see this as a Pyrrhic victory. Too, they are hard-working and will keep at a task until it is finished. In small ways they are very loyal to their friends, but if there is much pressure put on them, they will abandon friendship in favour of expediency. Responds well to praise or flattery, and through this can be led upwards or downwards in the world. They have an unhappy, but not a difficult life.

3 (Confirming). They are creative and artistic, but more through the appreciation of art than in its creation. Sometimes, they seem to be on the sidelines of things, but they enjoy the pleasure of others so much this doesn't seem to bother them. They are friendly and reliable and will not betray a confidence or promise. They are enthusiastic, happy, and generous, and their lives will be full wherever they live. They are family orientated, and most prefer to have a large number of children or an extended family of uncles, aunts, cousins, and family friends.

4 (Extending). Likely to be a pretty rough life, one largely lived in the service of others, but one with a strong and rich texture. These people do achieve a great deal, not for this lifetime, but for the next. They are involved with other people, and have a strong sense of loyalty. They get on with their work, making no great claims nor demanding much from others. They have a simple attitude to life, based on an essential ability to separate the important from the ephemeral or to concentrate only on the former. They are gentle people who will refuse to be imposed upon by others. They will, however, often face those who will try.

5 (Impediment). These people don't manage to set priorities in life; they will take on one task and, before it's finished, drop it in favour of another one. They do like other people, but have some trouble making the approach, getting to know people or getting to know them better. They are often accused of not taking responsibility, but it's more that they really don't know why others are taking offence at what they say or do. They are in many ways wrapped in a sort of cocoon where everyday facts just don't seem to reach them. They observe without really seeing, and unless they learn to do so, they will not lead a happy life, but one with a continual threshold of consternation and confusion.

6 (Confirming). A stay-at-home who makes home far more than a place to eat and sleep. These people make their homes an extension of themselves like the canvass is an extension of the painter. This person learns about the cycles of life and learns to live within them, making the most of good times and making the least of bad times. They neither look for too much nor accept too little, and this they find a formula for a happy life. They dislike the spotlight, and there are some rules that have to be obeyed by everyone, and from these rules they will live a happy, quiet life.

7 (Impediment). These people are characterized by isolation from others. They are torn between seeking higher things and greater principles and seeking simple, human companionship. They would do better to seek the latter, for only there will they find the harmony they see as so lacking in the world. They are tinged with a knowledge of the *weltschmertz,* or worldsorrow. Their homes are often slightly lacking in human warmth as they get themselves wrapped in the idea of changing the whole world, all at once. Unless they turn to their fellows first, their considerations of the sublime will lead them to misery and confusion.

8 (Extending). These people are quiet and reserved; people who separate the world from their home life, and see the distinction as a very clear border. They will be touched by tragedy in their lives, but they will rise above it. In their home lives they are dedicated, fiercely loyal to friends, passionate with lovers and ideas alike. Little wonder they need a place to relax and feel at ease, they throw themselves utterly into so many things they have to have a place to rest and recharge. They also like light comedy and the fine arts as a means of unwinding. On the whole, they lead an intense but not, by their own standards, hard life. However, their own standards, when placed upon others, often gives them the image of a hard taskmaster.

9 (Confirming). These people love their homes, and love travel just as much. They reconcile this with souvenirs or nostalgia, but however much they like one, the other will pop its head up eventually. They see life as a struggle to live by the eternal principles of liberty, justice, and self-betterment, but admit that even they don't manage to do this

as often as they should. They admit the discrepancy between the ordered heavens and the chaos that often marks life on earth, but still believe that by responsibility (right thought and right action), harmony (sound mind and sound body) will result. These people are energetic, and visionary and likely to go far in life. Their own life will be just and quiet, with a measure of real achievement to it.

Destiny Number 7 and Name Number

1 (Confirming). A seemingly contradictory personality characterizes these people. They are interested in the new, but are fiercely loyal to tradition, they are dynamic and yet reserved. Yet they see themselves as consistent and will not compromise their principles, though they will go far to avoid situations where such a compromise is necessary. They will lead a hectic life, but something of them will still find time to contemplate and, in fact, to calculate. These are people whose material actions are done in the service of their metaphysical principles.

2 (Trial). These people are easily influenced on the large questions of life, for the hubbub of life has captured them. It is not that they themselves are party goers, but they believe that that is the proper role model of life, and there is no other. They should consider the long term of things more, and take more store by the source of things, to which they actually have a strong link. These people do good work when they can, and are friendly to others, if a bit shy. Because of this shyness, they tend to be a bit impressionable, taking the ideas and attitudes of others as their own. Similarly, it makes them easy to upset, though they themselves are not actually nervous people. But unless they team up with someone with good analytical abilities, they will find life a jumbled, head-long confusion.

3 (Trial). They are energetic, enthusiastic, and somehow ill-equipped for the long moments of silence introspection requires. They don't actually deny the importance of karmic tasks or of destiny, but they do believe any obligations they have can be put off indefinitely. So, though their lives begin favourably enough, by middle age it has dropped well and truly into the muck. They are very creative, being able both to come up with their own ideas and to be able to tap into

the universal storehouse, but when they try to put the plans into practice, they tend to backfire. These failures can embitter them and make them moody or morose. They tend to blame these failures on other people, rather than realizing that after you have finished your karmic tasks then you can go your own way for a while. Admit that much, and their lives will become much easier and happier.

4 (Confirming). These are people who accept the importance of the spirit, but start by building a solid material foundation from which to make studies. The image of a Medieval alchemist, financing his studies by being a chemist or doctor. They are honest and demanding, patient and careful, and probably very lucky in making money. They dislike ceremonial roles, and are much more inclined to be kingmakers rather than king, because to them it is effect and not credit that is the crux of the matter. These people will lead a good, steady life, more concerned with their own pursuits than the pursuits of the world around them.

5 (Extending). A combination that would seem a mismatch in one person. Seemingly quiet and reserved, never one of the gang, they still know everything that is going on. Yet, in other contexts they are party going, enthusiastic, boisterous, and adventurous. They make good confidants, in that they don't reveal secrets, but seem to home in and reveal to others secrets that haven't been told to them. They make minor decisions quickly, but sleep on major decisions. They listen to new ideas, but test those ideas more harshly than those already in place. This makes change slower, but makes certain every single change is for the better. Time is a tester for these people, for though they have an almost golden age in youth, in later years they often resent what was left uncompleted or what is still remaining to be done.

6 (Impediment). These are people who have an image of the irredeemably spoiled self. Their insights into the universe provide a fodder for manipulating others. They, themselves, are unstable people, seemingly bound up with others but always keeping some reserve from them. They lack any knowledge of the cycles of life, and blame others for any failings of their own. The image to keep in mind for them is the mad Roman Emperors like Caligula and Justinian. They often

succeed in damaging things by sucking up to those who are susceptible to flattery.

7 (Confirming). Like all cases where D.N. and N.N. coincide, this configuration accentuates the best and worst of the number, but inclines to help towards the best. These are people who have a true insight into the spiritual laws of the universe. Their lives are sometimes filled with action and determination as they test the material world, and later life is contemplative and somewhat austere. However, they are warm and friendly people even though they present a special reserve. Their trouble is they don't know how to present these truths to the world, certainly not in a world dominated by Western and scientific materialism.

8 (Impediment). Determined, ruthless, efficient, cunning, and letcherous, one might think they are likely to set the world on fire. But they are also sporadic in their activities and inclined to that sort of fantasy where they tackle things far too large for themselves. Thus, though they have many plans, they never seem to arrive where they want to go. They fail, simply, to see the nature of the universe, they don't understand how things are connected together, so their plans never follow along in smooth patterns. They therefore lead hard and painful lives from their mid- to late-twenties on. In youth, when action more than achievement applies, this is not much of a problem, but when it comes to establishing themselves in a career, the problem becomes a crisis. Only if they strip everything down and start again from first principles will they put their lives back on track.

9 (Extending). Their early lives are probably going to be rough, and a lost parent is not beyond probability. This early knocking gives way in later life to solid achievements in home and career. Convinced right can win, they set about proving it by implementing their strong sense of justice in their own affairs. They are people who have insights into the universe, though not necessarily the ability to bring those insights to ground level for other people. These are people of contrasts; sometimes egotistic, other times self-effacing, a traveller in body and soul who believes in the family as the centre of society, dynamic and contemplative, pious and cynical. They are people with a sense of

the limitations of themselves and the world they live in, and are subject to disappointment in their later lives.

Destiny Number 8 and Name Number

1 (Extending). These people are determined, active, optimistic, logical, and intuitive. They have a good battery of assets with which to face the world. There is some struggle in them between a belief in organization and individual as the most important aspect of life, and will often vascilate on this. It can also make them change career several times in their lives. They will live a hard, happy life, but one with egotism touching at its edges. They can be very opportunistic with people and situations, for there is something of a primitive hunter in them. It also makes them believe bailing out can be the better part of valour, and this is one black mark on their characters to watch out for. But if they control that they do fairly well in life.

2 (Confirming). They are loyal to people more than processes, and prefer to think of what will get the job done than what is the correct-by-the-manual method of doing things. They love people around them and consider the home to be of prime importance. They are likely to settle down early in their lives but, they are likely to have an affair or two on the side — or possibly in the middle, there is some consideration of open marriage in these cases. They make decent leaders, but only if the situation is normal. In a crisis they can vascillate and need consultation too much to be effective. They lack the daring that would sometimes be useful to them. In all, they will lead quiet, happy lives in which most of their desires will be fulfilled.

3 (Trial). They are too easily distracted and too in love with having a good time now to achieve much. When they try to remain aloof, they fail, and when they try to join in, they feel guilty. To try to become one of the group, they listen to others' secrets and then forget to keep the secrets. They have little love of the home, and are generally unattracted to long term relationships. They live for the moment, but the moment eludes them, because they somehow have in the back of their minds the importance of what other people think of them. In youth they are often left on the outside of things, in middle age

they are often the fifth wheel in the group. In all, a disappointing sort of life which could be reversed if they would think more about what they are doing.

4 (Trial). Meticulous and organized when there is no pressure on, they tend to go to water in the crunch. They dislike leading others, or being led themselves. They prefer to withdraw into the home or the familiar, for they have a feel:ng of 'what's the use?' which grows more intense as life goes on. They tend to make up for their failings by heaping blame onto other people. These people are often prone to a particular hate upon which they fix the ills of the world. They are ambitious, but do not realize it takes effort to have all the nice things they have seen other people have. If they would be less sedentary, less involved with their own ruts, their lives would not be so unhappy, and they would stop boring everybody else in sight.

5 (Confirming). These people are active and alert, seemingly jumping from one thing or another. But they keep a mental notebook going so it doesn't all become too much. Sometimes the notebook doesn't work, and then it's usually family and personal pleasures that have to give way to business. At other times, though, they are not people who will sacrifice themselves or their families on the altar of business/politics/whatever. They see organizations as serving human beings and won't let it flow the other way around. Ambitious, they have to be careful of the sin of pride. They spend their early lives laying the groundwork for what they want to do; not a haphazard search in which they use what they learn, they seem to start out with a general idea of what they will do. In middle life they consolidate, and in later ages wrap up and look over what they have achieved. They are loyal to others and have a long list of friends, but in the end prefer to work alone.

6 (Extending). These are careful, meticulous people who keep a long range plan in mind and work to it. They are traditionalists who don't like to see things changed, and to them the family and the home is the centre of life. They have a strong dynastic urge, but don't tend to suffocate their children. They are friendly, charming hosts who enjoy

putting on parties. They have a natural understanding of the value of harmony and responsibility, and from that find the principle of interlockingness easy to grasp, but sometimes very difficult to apply. They are loyal to friends, but steadfast in opposing what they see as wrong. They make steady, appreciative, but somewhat unimaginative lovers. Their early lives are actively centred until about late middle age, when they turn the reigns over to someone else.

7 (Impediment). Gossip and malicious lies can often be the meat of their social lives, for they take no responsibility. Quick to respond to threat or potential threat, they don't lay plans for the future. As they get older this can become a serious problem. They suffer from these actions, but often think it unjust that the universe should seem to turn on them. Impractical, they want to see things changed, but don't bother to find out how to do so. They offer 'grand solutions' to the world's problems but never take even the first step to bringing them about. Despite this they can make some lasting friendships which can help show them where they have gone wrong.

8 (Confirming). Best summed up as a deadly enemy and a good friend, these people are a bit reserved but friendly, magnanimous, and loyal. However, they have no tolerance for cruelty or injustice, and though they don't bear grudges, they are implacable enemies until the armistice is signed. Then they forgive and forget. Their concern in life is to build an organization, to systematize what is chaotic, to make regular the ad hoc. They lead what seems to others a hard life, but to them is merely an intense one.

9 (Impediment). These are people who tend to show great promise early on in life but then peter out in middle age. They have a depth of vision and organizing skills, but lack the sort of human warmth necessary for any real enterprise to be completed. Shrewd observers, they are open to flattery. They make friends easily but tend to go cold on them again. They should take stock of themselves, and overcome their sense of the glorious I which makes them believe themselves the most important things in the universe. They need to know their limits, to be able to take things one step at a time.

Destiny Number 9 and Name Number

1 (Impediment). Gregarious and fun-loving, they have tempers that are rarely far from the surface. They are consumate egotists, gamblers who go for the big risk, big return bet. They often lack courtesy, and they enjoy a large party more than an intimate dinner, activity-centred parties more than people-centred parties. Where they penetrate the principles of the universe, they apply their knowledge to their own ends. They do have some friendships, and extending the give-and-take principles to other people could help them tremendously. It could help them overcome a deep-seated fear of other people. If this doesn't happen, then they will probably die alone.

2 (Extending). Vigour, gentleness, knowledge, and wisdom combined. Yet, they can be impractical, leading these people into ineffectual but happy lives. They should remember that people who do little are not so much widely liked as not widely disliked. When faced with injustice or impiety, they withdraw rather than fight, believing it will collapse on itself. Family orientated, they are friendly, trustworthy, and loyal people who manage to keep things going in an extended family. They have a wide circle of friends and are willing to lend a hand when the time comes. These are people who understand the importance of the feeling of community.

3 (Confirming). They are friendly, amusing, and games loving, a true asset to a gathering, large or small. They are quick thinkers, though they often appear unconventional. Intuitive, they have logic to back this up, and many actions which seem spontaneous are planned out beforehand. There is a manipulative side to them, for they are curious about everything and that includes human behaviour. They are often good investors, and are willing to share advice or whatever they have with friends. They live comfortable lives, but tend to face a great deal of opposition late in life. In early life they tend to be happy-go-lucky and seemingly approved of by one and all.

4 (Trial). Though they have a visionary nature, they are hyper-critical, picking the vision apart under a welter of organizational detail, rules and regulations. They are people who lack confidence in themselves

and in others. They embroider things, trying to disguise the simple, and assume others do the same thing. Thus, though they have a wide circle of acquaintances, they are unlikely to have anything like true friends. Nevertheless, they are hard-working and in many ways loyal people who would be unwilling to do anything that would actually harm anybody. However, they are not self-starters. They will finish what they are told to do but they won't look for further work. They would do well to introspect and accept what is truly there. Truth is the way to happiness.

5 (Trial). These people are all show and no reality. They talk of wisdom, of the right way to do things, but in the end it means nothing to them. They are eloquent, but they are also fools. They are likely to have easy childhoods and rough lives in old age, with the middle being pretty variable. When things go against them, they turn petulant and angry. They delight in the pains of others, however, and will make great humour of other people's misfortunes. They jump from thing to thing, because they are looking for the easy way to do things, and there isn't necessarily an easy way. It's the same with people they meet, they tend to drop people as soon as the novelty wears off, but resent being dropped, first.

6 (Confirming). They are introspective but not unworldly. These people are truthful, gregarious, and happy, but they very much need time to themselves and always keep a part of themselves separate from what is going on around them. They are willing to help, but not if it's a lost cause. They have a strong attachment to both the home and travel, but the former takes a strong hold early in life. These people travel in the soul more than the flesh. They are people who lead quiet lives of principle rather than the fads of the moment. Their families are important to them, but in the end not as important as those principles, for they are absolutely intolerant of greed, hypocrisy, false pretences, and especially of uncontrolled lust.

7 (Extending). Observant and cheerful, they are in many ways tight-lipped. They often seem slightly detached from the home and divorce at least once is a real possibility. Yet, they have a strong sexual nature

and provide lively if not necessarily experimental sex. They also have a pious streak, seeing everybody as part divine and part mortal, and realizing the mortal part is a bit of a joke. This gives them a good humour and an ability to laugh at themselves. Slightly ascetic in their own lives, they still begrudge no one else any luxuries. They thus lead hard lives, but lives that achieve much for others.

8 (Impediment). They believe the vision lives solely through them and therefore they can change the vision around as they like. With such overwhelming spiritual ambition, it isn't surprising that they are people who promise much and deliver little, people who are both devious and petty. They never forget a slight, but equally, avoid giving slights. They try to get as much as they can from a relationship, digging into other people for favours, but they will never carry on this activity until the relationship breaks. Though they can keep at a job they don't like for years, churning out decent work all the while, if there isn't a component of survival involved, they have little patience and can abandon a project as soon as the first wave of enthusiasm is over. The first part of their lives is emotionally satisfying but materially frustrating, the second part is materially satisfying and emotionally frustrating.

9 (Confirming). They are visionaries, travellers in mind and, as long as the money holds out, body. They will have a vision of what they want to do with their lives, and from about late twenties on will begin to put it into effect. Before that time, they are explorers of themselves and the world around them. Good natured, friendly, loyal to those around them, but they still have a bit of an ego, and tend to believe they were made for great things. This can make them slightly patronizing of others. More than most harmonious relationships of D.N. and N.N., these people need a partner who will smooth out their rough edges, and usually they find one early in life. They will, however, have a couple of severe disappointments in their love lives, though relatively few in their sex lives. In all, they lead pretty good lives, in which actions and achievement are given in an admirable mix.

CHAPTER NINE

SUCCESS THROUGH NUMEROLOGY

It is still possible to buy numerology books which swear you will be lucky on certain days or with certain numbers and, by gambling on those numbers on those days, you can get rich. Frankly, you would do as well to think about finding out the lucky number of the horse or the jockey as your own, and in either case, it doesn't help. There is no replacement for simply working for success. All numerology does is point out opportunities you would otherwise miss, and to smooth out many of the humps along the way. In the end, it becomes 10 per cent inspiration, 80 per cent perspiration, and 10 per cent numerology. This chapter is about that last 10 per cent.

There are a number of methods by which numerology can help you to be a success in life. It can help you get where you want to go, and I've chosen four methods here and provided them in outline form. They aren't hard and you should be able to put them into practice more or less right away.

Change Your Name
This is the most popular method with numerologists, and almost every book on the subject has a chapter on it. Simply, if your Name and Destiny Numbers are disharmonious, you are going to have problems in life. To cure that, change your name as a means of changing your response to the universe's demands on you, and in that way become successful.

It's a common fallacy that this change will be within days, in fact there is always a sort of backlog of karmic debts or bad habits that have to be cleared first. This may seem unpalatable but it is still true.

Worse, if you don't change, the backlog doesn't get cleaned out and only becomes bigger.

You may want to change your entire name by deed poll, but this isn't always necessary. Just check in the numeroscope which name variants don't fit the Destiny Number and change those variants.

For example, if you have a Destiny Number of 5 and you've been calling yourself Fred (a 6) or Freddie (also a 6) you might want to change your Personal Name so it fits with the Destiny Number rather than form an Impediment to it. You could change your name to Rick (5) rather than, say, Frederick (7) or something else. Since Rick can be said to come from Frederick, this presents no real problems, and would make the Personal Name Number Extending to the Destiny Number.

Now, take a look at the Formal Name. Like the Personal Name, it is fairly easy to change. Not quite as easy in some ways — Personal Names can often be nicknames — but with a lot of leeway around. There are an incredible number of titles, variations, initials and shortenings of names you can use when you sign things. Fortunately, few people care about the name on the cheque so long as it doesn't bounce.

Take the example above. Rick could keep the Formal Name Freddie Smith or Fred Smith if that's how he used to sign forms. Both come out to a 3 and this Extends Destiny Number 5. If he wants, he can change the name to Rick Smith, but only because that comes out to a 2, and this is Confirming to the Destiny Number. If it didn't come out to a suitable number, the Formal Name and the Personal Name would have to be a bit different. But, suppose his Full Name is Frederick Ajax Smith, that is, a 4 name. Then there could be some real need to change the name by deed poll or some other legal method. You could, for example, change the name by changing the first or middle name, or by adding another middle name. This alone would give you a great deal of room to manoeuvre. So Frederick Ajax Smith could change into Frederick Ajax Joseph Smith and his Full Name Number would be 5, which is the same as his Destiny Number. This would in most countries require very little legal work.

Just remember, if you want to change your name, to start with rough details, and flesh out the matter as you narrow things down to a short list. Keep in mind it will be your name, so it has to be pleasing to you, something you can wear every day of your life. But keep detailing out the numerological side as well, until only the best possible influences are retained.

It is effectively impossible to come up with a numerologically 'perfect' name, but make as close an approximation as you can. Then begin using your new name with friends, relatives, and so on. Change your bank signature (you will not in most cases have to change the bank or account name as well) and so on. Within three weeks to three months you will begin to change as your new name becomes your correct numerological description.

The Cycles

Remember we talked about the cycles of destiny and how each date has a particular influence on your life? If you are like most people, you took it in a passive way, thinking about what each sort of cyclic day would mean to you. But in this case, think about turning it all around. Suppose you planned out what you were going to do, or even what you expected to happen to you by the influences guiding that particular date.

In a way, salespeople do this all the time. Many won't approach new customers on Friday afternoon or even all day Friday, but just go and see customers they already have just to 'see everything's going all right'. Simply, it's not the right day in the weekly business cycle for new projects.

In the same way, use the cycles. Take a calendar and map out for the next five years the sorts of cycles you will be facing on each date. From that, plan your activities and goals around those days when your cycles will be most conducive to your success. So go back and re-read the chapter on cycles with this purpose in mind.

Success Maps

Success can be reduced to numbers just as easily as your name (success: 611/8). It's the same as love (495/9), power (725/5), a car (94/4), a friend (164 / 2) or anything else you can possibly imagine. Anything and everything is reducable to numbers and can therefore be influenced by numbers. What you have to do is set out the goals and constantly refine and hone them until they are more and more specific, compact, and clear. Then you can learn their numerological influences and use them to get those goals for yourself.

When you've set your goals, set the cycle dates by which you will get them. At this stage don't worry about the hows and wherefores of the things, you only need to set the goals, other things will work it all out for you. What you need is compatible cycle dates. To get these, you have to take into account your Destiny and Name Numbers.

For example, suppose you have a 3 Destiny Number and a 6 Name Number and what you want is a luxury car. Luxury and car are each 4, so it should be attained on a date when something suitable is available.

But, if you don't have any car, you have to set a date for getting a car. Then you have to start in on the adjectives. It's a matter of fact that once you have the noun of the goal, the adjective becomes more and more important as you move up a 'ladder' to what you ultimately want. So from car you go to family car to new car to expensive car to luxury car. You just keep moving up the ladder choosing dates appropriate to each stage.

Of course, some things aren't differences in a ladder. A country residence is a country residence (and is 8/1). If this is your goal and your Destiny Number is 2 and your Name Number is 3, you might have some trouble due to those Impediments; 2 to 3 and 1 to 2. In this case, the person should pick a cycle with 5 dominant, since 5 is Confirming to 8 and 2 and Extending to 3 while being Trial only to 1. The weakness, of course, is in that Trial one, and the person would have to keep the ideals of the place within self-control. Even so, expect a mortgaged or rented property, or one that can only be used on weekends or possibly even one that needs a lot of work. It would again be up to a new cycle date for those latter problems to be resolved in the person's favour.

How do you know which dates to choose? Simply look to the noun or adjective (depending what stage you are on now) and choose the date with the greatest potential. Prefer Confirmation to Extension, Trial to Impediment.

The only real trouble is that on any one day you will have a daily, monthly, and yearly cycle, the Destiny and Name Numbers, and probably a noun and adjective number as well. It is not easy. It can only be done by taking it in steps. If you have started by making your Destiny and Name Numbers compatible, so much the better.

Start with the Destiny Number, and work out harmonious numbers. Fit all your Name Numbers in with this. Make certain the cycle numbers match the Destiny Number and the corresponding Name Number. In other words, the daily cycle should be compatible with the Personal Name Number, the monthly cycle with the Formal Name Number, and the yearly cycle with the Full Name Number. Anything more than this proving compatible is a bonus, and you can't even always get this much within a reasonable length of time.

From there, work out your goals and their numbers. Work out with that, how it will affect your life. If you want a car, say you want it to make your personal life more convenient, you would be looking to find a daily cycle compatible with your Personal Name. If the same car were to make your business more successful, it would be necessary to find a monthly cycle harmonious with your Formal Name.

Of course, most goals take in more than this. You will spend more than a little time choosing appropriate periods and dates for each sort of goal. Over time it becomes automatic. Initially, however, you will do well to spend a lot of time figuring out why you want various things.

If, like most of us, you want some things for a variety of reasons, you should spend a lot of time finding those dates which have supreme compatibility with each of your Name and Destiny Numbers. Build your major goals in life around these and let the others fall into place from there.

Partners
If you want love or a business partner, numerology has effective advice to offer. In this, you use the same tools as used in examining the numeroscope of an individual, plus several others. The most important is examining parallel positions in the chart.

For example, people with harmonious Destiny Numbers are more likely to have a long relationship than those with disharmonious Destiny Numbers. The sort of relationship it will be, happy, tempestuous, and so on, is discovered through the Name Numbers.

Here the area of life is the same as described when dealing with individual charts: the daily life is described by the Personal Name, the business, social and political life by the Formal Name, etc. If the Name Numbers are harmonious on any level, then the relationship will be fruitful on that level. Disharmony marks any area of problems, strife, and confrontation. It is from this that you can judge how to deal with a person, and how well you can get to know that person.

So, if one person has a Destiny Number 3 and the other has one of 4, they are not likely to have a long-lasting relationship if left to their own devices. Naturally, they may in this society be forced to keep associating, in work being a prime example. If this is the case then the two will become cordial and distant, building up a wall between them so that, though in physical proximity, they have spiritually gone separate ways long ago.

On the other hand, if one person has a Destiny Number of 4 and the other a Destiny Number of 6 or of 7, then there is likely to be an enduring relationship. If their Personal Name Numbers are 6 and 9 respectively, then they will have a harmonious and happy relationship in day-to-day life. But, if their Formal Name Numbers are 1 and 9 respectively, then they would do well to stay out of business partnerships.

If you are to be successful, you will some time or another have to deal with other people. Numerology gives a good entré to knowing people. But, suppose you want to know someone for a particular purpose. Would they be a good spouse, business partner, or lover? These, too, can be explored through the numeroscope.

Begin by exampling the type of relationship you want as a goal. Like anything else, it can be reduced to a number, and that number can be fitted into your system of cycles. The problem is, the other person has a system of cycles, too. What you must do is find a date in which you and they are willing to enter the style of relationship you want. In other words, the date must be compatible with the appropriate Destiny and Name Numbers of two people and the goal of the exercise.

There are a lot of influences to mix and match, but it can be done. When you have chosen the goal, choose both an appropriate starting date (when you begin your campaign) and conclusion date (when you make your offer). This can be highly useful in business, when you can know when to begin a sales campaign and when to try to get them to sign on the dotted line.

Take an example. Two people, one with a Destiny Number of 3 and the other of 5. They want to have a relationship that is an affair, plain and simple. So they are looking for a 5 style relationship. Since they work in the same office, they would be looking to settle on one another as prospects on a cycle date where the influences are Extending to their Formal Names and Confirming to their Personal (short affair) or Full (long affair) Names. They should then consumate their relationship on a cycle date Confirming to their Formal and Extending to their Personal of Full (same notes) Names. In this way they will have chosen the most auspicious dates.

Look, then, for a cycle date of, say, 5 if their charts ran like this.

	A	B
Destiny No.	3	5
Full Name	9	7
Formal Name	3	2
Personal Name	5	8

Obviously, these have been chosen to show how much compromise is necessary. The cycle 5 Confirms the intent and Extends A's Formal Name while being Trial to B's Formal Name. So in this case, A had better do the advancing. If the cycle number were 4, B would have to take the first steps. Better yet, they might like to try a 9 cycle date, which is Confirming to A's Formal Name and Destiny Number while Extending to B's Formal Name though Trial to the Destiny Number.

There are innumerable permutations to this. Try working out the steps of this relationship and the sort of cycle dates appropriate to taking each step. The same can be done for two people who want to start a business. Then the same for two people who want to go on a trip together. When you can do that, you will have all the basics. After that it's just a matter of practice.

Summary

We have looked at four of the methods by which numerology can help you become a success. We have ignored things such as talismans, spells, and meditations which, while helpful, and while they may be influenced by numerological principles, are not in themselves numerological.

I want to stress that, to be successful, you will have to integrate the methods mentioned above. It's always better to have as much on your side as possible.

CHAPTER TEN

BEYOND NUMEROLOGY

Throughout this book we have dealt with a great many techniques and measurements of numerology. It has been no more than a brief introduction to the topic, however. After all, if numerology were as government-funded as, say, economics, the literature would be as vast and probably far more useful. With this book alone, you can begin to explore parts of the world that you probably thought were barred to you forever. You can begin to realign yourself with the forces that created and still guide the universe towards greater happiness, knowledge, and success.

If you carry on with things long enough, though, you will begin to perceive something beyond the words and descriptions, something beyond the very notions of the numbers themselves. It's as if, rather than understand about the numbers or the forces that created them, you perceive these forces directly. You begin to breach the gap between human words and the ineluctable truth they always try, and yet always fail to hold.

There are people who seem to rise above the effects of numerology in exactly the same way that there are people who don't seem to fit their sociological or psychological backgrounds. I don't believe we should find this too surprising.

Remember I described the alphabet and the words we use as moulded by society over many generations to fit its needs. This being so, there are people who soar beyond mere society, go beyond even civilization, which each society aspires to yet rarely achieves. These people are rare and not always known and to join their ranks is no small or easy task.

I don't believe the fact that numerology does not describe them is a failure of numerology, or that psychology's failure to describe them is a failure of psychology. There is always something of the ineluctable in some people, or at least something beyond eluctable truth. Whatever words we use, we will fail to capture all the truth of any matter in any subject. This being so, I should leave you with an understanding not only of numerology, but the limits of that knowledge.

Remember that numerology does not describe the background of an individual, their environment, or their education. These matter more in psychology and sociology. Numerology deals with how people utilize what they have rather than how much they have. Thus, a conservative, a liberal and a socialist who all have the same Destiny Numbers and Name Numbers are seen as akin by the numerologist. In the same way, the poor child and the rich, the educated and the uneducated are seen as akin if they have the same numerological influences.

To some this may seem nonsense, but I can argue the more conventional social sciences miss much of the picture. After all, if numerology says you have an abiding curiosity, this allows us to make some predictions about you. That you have been educated to PhD level, or have never even learned to read or write is, of course, very important, but less important than we might think. After all, if you are uneducated, you can still be curious. You can have enough degrees to wallpaper a room and still have a square head, unconcerned about what goes on around you. The education, here, is less important because we have weighed the other facts. It is those facts that numerology (and for that matter, astrology) is most interested in.

Make no mistake about it, though it uses an occult or metaphysical philosophy, numerology (and, again, astrology) is a form of social science. I can't explain the whole reason for this, other than to mention that, as an experimental model, social sciences and hence social scientists must narrow the range of their observations as much as possible, while also keeping their theory of what it all means to one system.

Take an example, a psychologist analysing dreams cannot look at a patient's dream and say, 'Sounds Jungian, but that little bit over there sounds Freudian, and that other bit sounds Behaviourist.' The theory of dream interpretation must be unified.

In the same way, a numerologist may accept that other schools of thought exist, but must maintain his or her own methods intact. You cannot analyse a Name Number and use the Ulian systemata for every letter but W, which looks like it ought to be Pythagorean. Nor can you make an exception in one interpretation and say that, though every other time 4 will have a certain interpretation, this time you will change it around a bit. This is not numerology, and it is not a form of social science.

A major difference between numerology and astrology from other social sciences, though, is that their concern is not with the 'vertical' divisions, such as between liberals and conservatives, but the 'horizontal' distinctions. In this, persons at the top and the bottom of different hierarchies are treated as alike.

Naturally this and the philosophy have combined to make very different methods of study and draw different conclusions. For example, numerologists and astrologers are more concerned about the same person throughout his or her life than is a sociologist, psychologist, or economist. Our samples are smaller, but are followed through for longer periods — hopefully for the whole of a life-time.

Since the person we will know for the longest time is ourselves (especially in the present mobile society) it is introspection that provides the bulk of numerological data. However, we also have access to the studies of others, and there are many people we can observe for many years on end. Thus, numerology has a criterion for success, and a methodology. That other social sciences have kept us from legitimacy is, considering the differences between us and them, not all that surprising. Nor is it really to be lamented.

Social sciences are notorious for not cross-fertilizing each other. Sociology has added little to economics, economics nothing to psychology, and none of them have anything to do with numerology or astrology, and the latter two have very little to do with each other. Social science doesn't work like the hard sciences, and we don't have to demand entrance into the ivory tower to help humanity.

So where does that leave us? Where we were to begin with. We are trying to understand a truth either so complex or so simple that it eludes us. We are working towards a truth with tools (words, numbers, graphs, and human minds) pathetically unable to grasp the whole of it. We progress without getting nearer, and show our progress only by the relative improvement from our previous position.

Never think of numerology (or anything) as the whole of the truth. However, realize numerology is an invaluable tool for getting you closer to the truth, just as it will make your life better and your understanding of the world deeper. If you continue to practice, you will become proficient with numerology and realize its value to you and others. There is far more you can explore than we have touched upon here. And if you keep studying, you may help to bring us much further along in our quest for truth that we have managed in this book, and that would be wonderful.

INDEX

Also in this series . . .

UNDERSTANDING ASTRAL PROJECTION

Anthony Martin

Astral projection is the ability to move beyond the physical body, to explore a world 'out of the body'. Once mastered, the techniques of astral projection can be used at will to escape from the confines of the physical body, move vast distances through space, penetrate apparently solid matter and experience strange encounters on the infinite inner planes.

With this book as your guide, you can take your first steps on the strangest journey of your life — a trip beyond the body.

UNDERSTANDING THE I CHING

Tom Riseman

The *I Ching*, or Book of Changes, is a system of foretelling the future that has been in daily use in China for at least 3,000 years.

Now its subtle psychology and often uncanny ability to predict future events are made available to the general reader in this new introduction, providing a handy précis of how to consult the Oracle and enabling anyone to master basic interpretation of the 64 Hexagrams.

With this book and an attitude of respect, the timeless wisdom enshrined in the *I Ching* can be at your command.

HOW TO DEVELOP YOUR ESP

Zak Martin

'There is a universe of untapped power, an infinite resource within the psychic reach of every person.'

How to Develop Your ESP sets out in clear, easy-to-follow terms tried and tested techniques for developing ESP (Extra-Sensory Perception) in its many forms, including telepathy, precognition, dowsing, divination, clairvoyance, psychometry, psychokinesis and dream interpretation.

Whether you have ever thought you were 'psychic' or not, Zak Martin's programme will quickly help you develop your natural gifts to the full.

MEDITATION: THE INNER WAY

Naomi Humphrey

Meditation is a marvellous self-help tool for a wide variety of physical, emotional and psychological problems. Meditation: The Inner Way explains the basic techniques used by the many and varied systems of meditation and shows that these techniques can be easily learned and applied to your life today.

Using clear instructions, in plain language, and carefully selected exercises, Naomi Humphrey shows how meditation can be used as a powerful force for self-improvement.